"Ben Young...understands what nonreligious people need in the way of reasons to believe. He also knows *how* to present th┐ reasons. Readers will find in this book some of the best advi┌ ┐nned on introducing people to the Christian faith—wit┐ ┐le-ness, and respect."

—**Dr. Hugh Ross,** ┌
author┐ ┐os

"Ben Young has a gift for deconst┐ ┌┐ews of the world that permeate our culture and ┐ ┌┐ize that these views are really no challenge at all to th┐ ┌ faith."

—**William A. Dembski,** aut┐ ┌ of *The Design Revolution*

"The typical questions that arise in conversations between Christians and unbelievers are raised here...A simple-to-read playbook for the encounters that believers often face and fear."

—**Jim Tour, PhD,** researcher and professor
of chemistry, Rice University

Why Mike's Not a Christian

BEN YOUNG
with SARAH FUSELIER

HARVEST HOUSE PUBLISHERS

EUGENE, OREGON

Cover by Left Coast Design, Portland, Oregon

Cover photo © Photodisc Photography/Portraits of Diversity/Veer

Back-cover author photo © Donald (dk) Kilgore

"Mike's Barbecue" and "Back to Barbecue" are fictional illustrations designed to help the reader think through possible or likely situations. Names, characters, places, and incidents are products of the author's imagination. Any resemblance to actual persons, living or dead, is entirely coincidental.

WHY MIKE'S NOT A CHRISTIAN
Copyright © 2006 by Ben Young
Published by Harvest House Publishers
Eugene, Oregon 97402
www.harvesthousepublishers.com

Young, Ben.
Why Mike's not a Christian / Ben Young.
    p. cm.
Includes bibliographical references.
ISBN-13: 978-0-7369-1865-7 (pbk.)
ISBN-10: 0-7369-1865-5 (pbk.)
1. Apologetics. I. Title
BT1103.Y68 2006
239—dc22   2006002116

Printed in the United States of America

07 08 09 10 11 12 13 14 / VP-CF / 10 9 8 7 6 5 4 3 2

In memory of
G.B. "Buddy" Landrum
and
Rick Smalley

Acknowledgments

I want to thank Sarah Fuselier and Toni Richmond for making this book a reality. Sarah made the book flow and wrote the big debates between Mike and Josh. Toni championed this project from the get-go and made sure it went to press on time.

I also want to thank the late Gregory Bahnsen and Peter Kreeft, Paul Copan, Frank Harber, William Dembski, Hugh Ross, and Jim Tour for their great contributions to apologetics and to this book.

CONTENTS

Mike's Barbecue

• • • • • • • • • •

One Sunday afternoon Josh went to his favorite barbecue restaurant to eat what he considered one of the best brisket sandwiches on earth—the tenderest meat covered in sumptuous sauce on a toasted bun, with pickles, white onion, and loads of jalapeños. Even more appealing was the price—at $4.50 a pop, a great sandwich turns divine. So in he walked, Tums in tow.

Just as he made it to the counter he heard a familiar voice over his shoulder: "Hey, it's 'Josh,' right?" the voice asked.

Josh turned around and tried his best to conceal his disappointment: "Yes, how are you, Mike?" He'd been looking forward to an afternoon of anonymity, a time to just relax and not talk much, especially not to people from work.

"Oh, fine. How's that report coming along?" Mike asked.

"Almost done. What about yours?" Josh said, stifling a sigh.

Mike thought a second and then said with a chuckle: "It's the weekend—what am I doing talking about work?"

In relief, Josh let out that sigh he had stifled. *Maybe this won't be so bad,* he thought.

The two co-workers got their food at the same time and decided to join each other at one of the tables outside. Let's take a look at their conversation and see why heartburn ended up being the least of Josh's worries that day:

Mike: So why are you dressed up?

Josh: I went to church this morning.

Mike: Church? I didn't know you were religious.

Josh: Yeah, I've been a Christian for a long, long time.

Mike: Interesting. I had no idea you were a Bible-thumper. [He chuckles.]

Josh: Well, I'm not...I mean...I'm not into pushing my beliefs on others.

Mike: Good for you, man! I get so tired of those folks who feel the need to convert everybody. I think it just shows weakness on their part. People need to keep their religious views to themselves, don't you think?

Josh: Well, I'm not sure about that.

Mike: It just seems like they're afraid to stand alone—almost like they need affirmation for what they believe. We all have our own individual beliefs. What's true and right for one person isn't necessarily true for the next.

Josh: Hmm. So what do *you* believe?

Mike: I personally believe that if you're a good person, you're going to be all right, whatever your idea of "all right" is. We're all here just trying to do our best, you know? To me, it shouldn't matter what path you take. None of us really *knows* what the truth is anyway. And if there really is a God, I can't imagine him condemning people for not believing one particular way. That just wouldn't be fair. It makes me so mad when these self-righteous Christians claim they're the only ones going to "heaven." You say you're a Christian—do *you* really believe Jesus Christ is the only way to God?

Josh: Yes, I do.

Mike: So you would condemn all the Jews, Muslims, Hindus, and the rest of the moral population just because they don't see Jesus as the Son of God?

Josh: Well, yes. All those other religions are false.

Mike: So, bottom line, if I don't believe in all this Jesus stuff, then God, if he even exists, is going to send *me* to the ultimate barbecue pit?

Josh: If that's the way you want to put it, yes.

Mike: Actually, that's the way *you* put it with your narrow-minded view. I suppose now you're trying to convert me...to rescue me from my ultimate doom.

Josh: Well, maybe.

Mike: Ha! I thought you said you weren't into that sort of thing.

Josh: What sort of thing?

Mike: At the beginning of this discussion you said you weren't into pushing your beliefs on others, and now look what you're doing. It shouldn't surprise me—I've yet to meet a Christian who wasn't a hypocrite.

Josh: Now wait a minute. That's not fair, Mike—

Mike: What do you mean, "not fair"? I don't think it's fair when you Christians say the rest of us are wrong just because we don't believe what you believe. How can you be so arrogant as to claim that your way is the only way?

Josh: I just feel that what I believe is the truth, and I've put my faith in what the Bible says.

Mike: The Bible? I can't give credibility to a work that's been passed around and undoubtedly embellished through the years.

Josh: Well, that's your decision.

Mike: Look, Josh, any educated person knows the Bible isn't really true. Evolution proved that a long time ago. I've read my fair share of the Bible and, sure, we can glean a modicum of wisdom from its tales and proverbs—just like any other ancient writing—but do you honestly think all that stuff really happened? The Bible is basically a bunch of myths. My grandmother was a Christian, and she used to tell us stories from the Bible. Let me ask you: How is a talking donkey plausible? That one was my favorite.

Josh: First of all, I don't care what scientists say about evolution. Science has been an enemy of Christianity from the get-go—

Mike: Ha!

Josh: And second, the donkey really did talk. Haven't you ever heard of a miracle?

Mike: Miracles like that don't happen these days, and if they don't happen now, why would they have happened then?

Josh: People are miraculously healed of all sorts of diseases all the time.

Mike: They just got lucky, in my opinion. What about all the people who *don't* get healed—people who've got entire churches praying for them? Why wouldn't God heal them? That seems so arbitrary.

Josh: God is in control, and we have to be happy with whatever he chooses to do.

Mike: "God is in control," huh? Let me ask you, where was God on September 11? If he was really in control, why would he have allowed something like that to happen?

Josh: I don't know, but I do feel that he was there, comforting those in pain.

Mike: There you go with your *feelings* again. How can you rest your whole belief system on your subjective feelings, Josh? I feel the world is flat. How do you feel about that?

Josh: Everyone knows the world isn't flat. That's been proven wrong.

Mike: Proven by whom, those "enemy" scientists?

Josh: Come on, Mike...you know what I mean.

Mike: No, I don't know, and that's what really irks me. Josh, you are a bright guy and a hard worker. I just can't figure out why you would believe all this mess when you know rationally that it's not true. Why do so many Christians feel the need to park their brains every time they go to church or open the Bible? I just don't get it.

Josh: You see, Mike, that's your problem. It takes faith. Sure, all those questions about evolution, miracles, the Bible, and other people's religions bother me at times. So what? All those skeptics and doubters are wrong.

Mike: Prove it!

Josh: I can't prove it. I just know what I believe, and that's good enough for me.

Mike: I just can't believe in something that doesn't make sense rationally. Take Jesus, for instance. How could a man—a man like you and me—actually be God?

Josh: Well, don't you think Jesus was wise and moral, like God would be?

Mike: Yeah, Jesus was a good man, a great moral teacher—but God in the flesh? I just can't buy that.

Josh: Again, Mike, it just takes faith.

Mike: We live in a modern age with iPods, satellite TV, and camera phones—and how smart people like you can take this archaic blind leap of faith is beyond me. Speaking of blind, you spilled a little barbecue sauce on your tie there, Josh.

Josh: Thanks, Mike.

Have you ever had a conversation like that? In your opinion, who won this informal debate? I would say Mike came out on top here. He appeared to have a number of good reasons not to believe in God, the Bible, and Christ's claim to be "the way, the truth, and the life."[1] And Josh didn't seem to have the answers for this barrage of religious and philosophical questions. He wasn't ready.

Would you be ready to respond to questions about your own belief system? Yes, you do have a belief system (all of us do), regardless of what it may be.

I can remember talking with one of my friends in college who happened to be a Hindu. During the course of the conversation, we both realized I knew more about Hinduism than he did, and he had no way to defend his faith. We couldn't proceed any further with the discussion until he had gone and learned more about what he "believed." I don't know about you, but that is not the kind of situation I relish.

We all like a good debate over a grande mocha with Ella crooning in our ears, but when it comes to our primary belief system, a few quips we memorized in freshman humanities will not suffice.

The truth is, we should all be able to answer this question for ourselves: "What is the basis for my beliefs, and how do those beliefs affect the way I live?" As humans, it is so natural for us to think we have everything figured out. As Americans, we love to exercise our right to talk about it. We all like a good debate over a grande mocha with Ella crooning in our ears, but when it comes to our primary belief system, a few quips we memorized in freshman humanities will not suffice. That's what this book is about. It's about intellectual integrity, about honesty, and about getting real with what you really believe.

If you are like Mike, a sincere skeptic looking for some answers, then I'm glad you've picked up this book. In the following chapters, I will respond to the many questions Mike posed in this debate, and hopefully, you'll find these responses at least rational, if not altogether convincing. If you are more like Josh, a sincere Christian in need of some intellectual support, then I'm glad you're reading this as well. I hope you will 1) come to understand why some people reject the Christian faith and 2) learn how you can respond more effectively to their objections. In the final wrap-up, we'll take a trip back to the barbecue joint and see how Josh fares with more knowledge under his belt.

Part One

OKAY, WHY NOT?

Chapter 1

Because It's True for You,
But Not for Me

The little discussion between co-workers Mike and Josh in the opening chapter revealed a lot about their worldviews. Mike strongly believes that truth is relative and that any particular point of view is as valid as all other points of view. He thinks it should be up to the individual to decide what he or she considers truth. Josh, on the other hand, believes that truth is absolute and that Christianity is what leads us to that truth.

Much of their disagreement is an old war between those who believe in absolute truth and those who believe truth is relative. George Barna recently conducted a survey that showed 64 percent of American adults (18 years old and up) do not believe in absolute and objective moral truth.[1] If you concur with Mike and the 64 percent of Americans who take a relativistic stance, then please allow me to challenge you to rethink your claims.

Meet Frank and Carl. Frank owns a jewelry store; Carl is a

diamond thief. However, Frank isn't aware that Carl is a thief. It's a typical morning at the store, and at about 10 AM, Frank begins polishing some necklaces. Carl strolls in, feigning an interest in buying something for his wife. They talk about possible purchases, just as they've done every day for the past week. Then the topic changes:

Frank: You know, I was watching TV last night, and they had some religious fanatic on there. This wacky fundamentalist was saying he believes there is absolute truth. And, to top it off, he said he knew this absolute truth and was trying to impose his beliefs and his morality on everyone else. Now, that just doesn't make any sense to me. How can one man claim to *know* the truth? How can one man say he has all the answers? What arrogance!

Carl: Yeah, I know what you mean. I grew up in the church and heard that all the time. My mom was the worst... she was always trying to shove religion and the Bible down my throat. But, thank *God* (ha!), I've moved past all that.

Frank: I mean, everyone knows today that all truth is basically relative. It all depends on your culture and individual background. How can one culture say it's right and another is wrong? There is no absolute right and wrong. What truly enlightened person believes that?

Carl: I'm right there with ya, buddy.

Carl says he has a meeting and leaves yet again without making a purchase. He's been casing the joint for a week now, and tonight he's ready to make his move.

At 10 PM, he routinely makes his way past the alarm, without a glitch. He's got his ski mask and a Glock 33 (with a silencer), and everything is going as planned except for one thing—there's a light on in the back. *Frank's not usually here at this time; I need to make sure,* he thinks. He walks to the back and, sure enough, Frank is sitting there, paying bills.

In terror, he immediately yells out, "Hey, don't shoot... don't shoot...don't kill me...you can take whatever you want!"

Carl: That's exactly what I intend to do.

Frank: Hey, wait a minute. Don't I know you? I recognize your voice. You're Carl.

Carl: Frank, buddy, you shouldn't have done that. Now you've shown you know who I am, and if you know who I am, you'll turn me in, and if you turn me in, I'll have to go to jail, and I don't want to do that. So, Frank, it looks like I'm going to have to kill you.

Frank: You can't kill me! It's not right!

Carl: Wait, wait—what do you mean "it's not right"? You told me today you don't believe in absolute right and wrong. It depends on the individual, right? So, I'm going to have to kill you. I have no choice; I've got to look out for myself.

Frank: But I've got a wife and kids...I've got to take care of them.

Carl: Your wife and kids will get insurance money and will probably be better off without you. But what do I care about that anyway? I have to do this. I can't trust you, Frank.

Frank: Oh, you can trust me. Look, I won't turn you in. Trust me, please. Take everything I have...I don't care...please just spare my life.

Carl: Frank, you just don't get it. Remember our conversation today? Do you remember what you said—"There is no absolute right and wrong"? How can I trust you?

What does your word mean? Tonight it's right for you to say you won't turn me in, because it benefits you in this moment, but tomorrow it may be right for you to turn me in because you no longer have a gun to your head and you want your stuff back. Well, I'm doing what's right for me here. I'm not going to spend the rest of my life in the slammer, wearing an orange jumpsuit. I'm sorry, Frank. [He slowly squeezes the trigger, leaving Frank no time to recant his relativistic stance.][2]

DO THE RIGHT THING?

Now, this may seem like an extreme example to you, but indulge me a minute. If your motto is, "It's true for you, but not for me," then you've got to give Carl his due. You must give him permission to kill Frank. He has that right because self-interest rules the day in his mind. *That's a stupid story,* you may be thinking. *Anybody knows that killing is wrong.* Well, why is killing wrong? Why does an objective standard of right and wrong all of a sudden apply when it comes to murder? "I feel that it is wrong," you may say. But Carl felt it was right for him. You may then reply, "Well, it's against the law to steal and to kill. They voted and passed legislation about this. It's up to society to determine what's right or wrong." Okay, but what if I said to you that black people are inferior to white people and that a bunch of white people should take over the ships of the Royal Caribbean cruise line, go down to Africa, and bring some black people back with them to be their slaves?

By now you're really thinking I'm a nutcase because *everyone* knows slavery and murder are morally reprehensible. On what grounds, though? You just told me that society determines what is right and what is wrong—and just a while back in our nation's history, *society* said slavery was okay. *Society* also elected Adolf Hitler as Chancellor of Germany, giving him 90 percent of the popular vote. And after World War II, when the Nazis were on trial for exterminating nearly 12 million innocents (half of whom were Jews), their defense was that they never broke German law.

Don't you see that in saying I don't have the right to impose my beliefs on *you*, you are imposing your beliefs on *me* by telling me what I shouldn't do?

Does that sound like a reasonable defense to you? Should their heinous crimes have been dismissed under that kind of logic? Absolutely not. But you have no standard for objecting. You cannot oppose theft, murder, slavery, genocide, pedophilia, or anything else you would consider unjust as long as society or the law deems them acceptable. So if moral truth is merely a social construct, you inevitably will have oppression.

"Hitler's regime and slavery are two extreme examples," you may be objecting. "Nevertheless, we can take society out of it. My point is, no individual should impose his morals or religious values on another individual. You don't have the right to tell me what to believe." But don't you see that in saying I don't have the right to impose my beliefs on *you*, you are imposing your beliefs on *me* by telling me what I shouldn't do?

Before we drown in a sea of quasi-semantics, let me give you another scenario: There is a man jogging by himself through the park one night. As he passes through a more secluded area, he sees someone brutally raping a young lady. He says to himself, *Well, I don't agree with what this man is doing, but who am I to say that he's in the wrong?* You would likely say this is outrageous, but would a true relativist have any basis for condemning this jogger? I don't think so. After all, he was only respecting the values (or lack thereof) of the rapist.

Now, I'm not saying that all relativists stand for murder, oppression, and rape. In fact, I believe many relativists are philanthropic by nature. What I am saying is that they don't always realize the repercussions of their claims. The German philosopher Friedrich Nietzsche admitted these repercussions when he wrote,

> The obliteration of God—and therefore, all objective standards for truth and morality—would usher in an age of nihilism, the rejection of all objective meaning in value. All that is left is the will to power, by which only the fittest survive.[3]

What it comes down to is this: When you throw objective moral truth out the window, it's every man for himself, every woman for herself—and the individual freedom you intended is forfeited and replaced by chaos and abuse.

YOU SAY "TOMATO"...

To be sure, when you move from culture to culture there are certain norms that differ. For example, I lived in Mexico City during the summer of 1989, and I observed firsthand some major differences between Mexicans and Americans. In Mexico (at least at that time), you did not leave your parents' home until you were married—it didn't matter if you were rich or poor, young or old. In fact, to leave the family nest for any reason other than marriage was considered a disgrace. In the United States, however, children are encouraged to leave home after they turn 18 or graduate from high school. To continue to live with your parents well into your 20s is not an ideal situation for most Americans.

Much like the notion of cultural norms is the idea of preferences. For instance, I prefer mint-chocolate-chip ice cream, and perhaps you like vanilla. I like the Houston Astros, and maybe you are a dyed-in-the-wool Yankees fan. When I am referring to absolute truth, I am not referring to norms that vary from culture to culture, nor to personal preferences, both of which are legitimate.

NO ESCAPING THE TRUTH

In reality, we can say we're "true" relativists all we want, but when the chips are down and the gun is to our heads, we all believe in absolute truth. We shake our fists in anger at Osama bin Laden, at genocidal killers in Rwanda and Sudan, and at our English teacher for giving us a D because she didn't like the color of our skin.

Why? Because we know that there is a right and there is a wrong outside of anyone's personal opinions about it. Something in us cries out for justice. We can't escape it any more than we can escape our longing to have intimate connections with others. It's the way we've been created. Every person in every culture has been made in the image of God. Though we have become estranged from him and have distorted that image, it is still there. And written on that image, though faintly perhaps, is a conscience endowed with the absolutes of who God is and what he requires of us.

> **There's a part of us that is drawn to God because we have an innate need to be in a relationship with our Creator, yet there is another part of us that wants to run away from Him.**

Paul talks about this in the book of Romans. Here he is referring to the Gentiles, who did not grow up under the law as the Jews did:

When Gentiles, who do not have the law, do by

> nature things required by the law, they are a law
> for themselves, even though they do not have the
> law, since they show that the requirements of the
> law are written on their hearts, their consciences
> also bearing witness, and their thoughts now
> accusing, now even defending them.[4]

This passage affirms that, by nature, we know what's right in God's eyes even if we haven't had it spelled out for us in the law. Earlier, Paul writes,

> Since the creation of the world God's invisible
> qualities—his eternal power and divine nature—
> have been clearly seen, being understood from
> what has been made, so that men are without
> excuse. For although they knew God, they neither
> glorified him as God nor gave thanks to him, but
> their thinking became futile and their foolish
> hearts were darkened.[5]

These words hit the mark. We know what we are to do, but we don't always like to do it. God has revealed himself to us through our conscience, through nature, and through the Scriptures, but we don't want to bend the knee to him and acknowledge that he is in control. We want to run our own lives.

I struggle with this, and so does anyone else who's honest. There's a part of us that is drawn to God because we have an innate need to be in a relationship with our Creator, yet there is another part of us that wants to run away from him—a part that wants to create our own "truths" that fit into our own self-focused agendas.

GO TO THE SOURCE

Here's what Jesus says about truth: "*I* am the Way, the Truth, and the Life."[6] In other words, *he* is the source. Now, does this mean we can't find truth in other religions, or in "secular" songs and movies? Absolutely not. All real truth is God's truth, and he can—and many times does—speak that truth to us through all sorts of media. And because he is God, he can transcend what even the writer, artist, or producer may have originally intended.* That said, any "truth" that does not have its foundation in a knowledge of God will eventually turn in on itself. Relativism is a case in point.

Of course, everyone has the right to believe in anything he or she wants, but just believing in something doesn't make it true. For any group of people, for any family, for any community to survive, it must have universal absolutes. No one really lives their life in a relative manner. When you pick up the phone and order a pizza, and the person on the other end of the line says, "It will be delivered within 45 minutes," you expect that someone will drive to your house and deliver a pizza within that amount of time, don't you? But for a relativist to be consistent, he would have to say that it's up to the pizza guy to decide if that was really the agreement. That's just silly.

Not only is relativism an unlivable worldview, it is also self-contradictory. Isn't the claim that there is no absolute truth an absolute truth claim in and of itself? For this very reason, relativism is at best confusing and at worst deceptive. It may seem all-encompassing, but it is just as exclusive as any other religious or philosophical perspective. Someone who believes in relativism cannot help but be just as dogmatic as someone who espouses Christianity or any other religion. It's impossible to avoid being emphatic about our particular belief system because (hopefully) everything in our lives—our thoughts, decisions, and actions—is based on or affected by our beliefs.

All I'm asking for is a little consistency, a little integrity here, which is the same I ask of myself. If I claimed to follow Christ but lived my life as though I didn't—with absolutely no

---

* Technically, theologians have categorized three main ways God reveals truth to us:

  1. *General revelation.* This comes through our moral conscience.

  2. *Special revelation.* This comes specifically through Jesus and the Christian Scriptures.

  3. *Common grace.* This is what we're talking about here—what we receive through "secular" music and movies, and other beautiful and good things.[7]

conviction about it—you would think I was a huge hypocrite. And I would be. So if you really, truly don't believe in an absolute right or wrong, then you negate your ability to criticize or even compliment the way others live their lives, whether they are Charles Manson or Paul McCartney.

QUESTIONS TO THINK OVER

1. Before you read this chapter, what was your position on moral relativism? (In other words, did you believe in absolute truth?) Since reading, has your position changed? Why or why not?

2. What is your ultimate standard for morality?

3. Apply that standard to Nazi Germany and to slavery.

4. At the end of the scenario with Frank and Carl, do you think Frank had a leg to stand on in his argument with Carl, given his particular stance on morality?

Chapter 2

Because All Paths Lead to God

* * * * * * * * *

Several years ago I hopped a plane to Los Angeles to hear my brother's band play at the House of Blues on Sunset Strip. The House of Blues is one of the coolest music venues I have ever been to—the wood decor, the revolving stage, and the memorabilia everywhere make it a unique place to dine and listen to music.

When I sat down at my table I noticed that above the stage were various symbols representing many of the major world religions. There was a cross for Christianity, a Star of David for Judaism, and the crescent moon and star for Islam, to name a few, all forming an arch on the main stage. And above all these symbols was this phrase in large letters: "All Is One." It reminded me of something Oprah Winfrey once said: "One of the biggest mistakes humans make is to believe that there is only one way. Actually, there are many diverse paths leading to what you call God."[1]

This perspective, held by Oprah, Mike, and many in our

society, seems to promote humility by saying, "My way is no better than your way." Religious relativism, like moral relativism, is attractive to many people because it appears to be inclusive and embracing of all people of all faiths. Perhaps you adhere to some form of religious relativism and see it as a way to advocate peace in the midst of bigotry and prejudice. Let's take a look at this point of view and its implications. Does religious relativism in fact solve the problem of intolerance or, like moral relativism, does it end up creating the very thing it criticizes?

WHAT IS ULTIMATE REALITY?

Let's take a look at a classic illustration—the story of "The Three Blind Men and the Elephant." Imagine there are three blind men standing around an elephant, trying to figure out what it is. The first blind man grabs onto its leg and says, "Ah, the elephant is like a tree." The second blind man then comes and grabs hold of its tail and says, "No, no, you're wrong. The elephant is like a snake." Then the third blind man goes and leans on the side of the elephant. He says, "No, both of you are wrong. The elephant is not like a tree, nor is it like a snake. It is like a wall."

Relativists often use this illustration to suggest that all the religions of the world grasp only bits and pieces of the truth. In essence, those who hold to this view are saying that all people of faith are leaning up against the same ultimate reality or god but simply describe it in different ways, according to their various perspectives. If this argument were true it would certainly neutralize any of the absolute truth claims of Hinduism, Buddhism, Islam, Christianity, Judaism, or what have you. I would use this analogy if I were a religious relativist, because it does sound really humble. If we're really all blind, someone who says, "I am the Way, the Truth, and the Life," would appear to be quite arrogant.

But take a behind-the-scenes look at this story, and some simple questions begin to surface. For instance, who is telling the story, and what is his perspective? Obviously, the person telling the story is someone who can see the whole elephant. How else would he know that the three blind men are grasping only parts of it? How would he know that its leg is not a tree but only part of the elephant's body, or that the tail is merely the tail and not a snake, and so on? The storyteller is claiming to have an exclusive vantage point that allows him to see ultimate reality. In other words, he alone gets the big picture. He knows what the elephant is and what the blind men are trying to figure out.

All of a sudden, the storyteller doesn't sound so humble anymore, does he? You start asking a few questions, and you'll soon discover that his view is completely self-contradictory too. While he is claiming that there is not *one* correct path, he's establishing his own path, or understanding of it all, as the absolute standard.[2]

More on this shortly, but let's look at another popular way to describe religious relativism. It is what I like to call the "mountaintop analogy." God is at the top of a mountain, and everyone else is at the bottom. As there are many different ways to the top of a mountain—some more difficult or time-consuming than others—so there are many different religions that all lead to the same God.

Once again, though, we could ask the question: Who's describing this? How does he know all paths reach to the top of the mountain unless he, himself, is at the top? Just like the storyteller describing the three blind men and the elephant, he is claiming to have absolute knowledge.

While we're at it, let's push his claim a little further. Would this relativist really say every path leads to God? How about Hitler's? David Koresh's? The KKK's? Most would say these people are sociopaths and bigots, and I would have to agree. However, for a religious relativist to be consistent, he would have to say, "Yes, their ways lead to God as much as the next person's."

He's not going to say that, though. In Mike-like fashion, he'll say that what matters is being a "good" person. Well, where does the standard for what's "good" or "bad" come from if there is no such thing as absolute truth? He may say that standard is what we're taught. By whom, I'd ask. By our parents and teachers. Okay, where did they get it? Society. And remember where society took us in chapter 1—to Nazi Germany and slavery.

WORLD RELIGIONS 101

You know, I would agree with Mike that there are a lot of good people who are Jewish, Hindu, Muslim, Buddhist, and Christian. I think you can find, as you survey the different religions of the world, moral people from all different faiths. I would also say there are some definite similarities in the moral codes taught by the various religions. But there are also some radical differences.

I was at a Burger King one time talking to a man about different world religions—he happened to be a Muslim. I say "happened" because his calling himself a Muslim seemed arbitrary, given the fact that in the course of our conversation he was mainly trying to explain to me that Islam, Christianity, Buddhism, and Hinduism are essentially teaching the same thing. And as I have talked to many people from different parts of the world, I have found that this assumption—that all religions are basically the same—often goes unchallenged. However, this Burger King, or "Have it your way," theology is especially prevalent in the United States, with our democratic mentality.

Here's the problem: If you buy into that assumption, then what that will do is weaken your particular faith (if you claim one), as well as cause you to be ignorant about the differences between various faiths. Now, let me clarify something right away and say that I'm all about harmony. I recently went to a U2 concert and watched Bono parade around the stage with a bandana on his head that said, "Co-Exist." In the middle of it all, he made reference to the fact that Christianity, Judaism, and Islam all look to Abraham as a key figure in their faiths. His point was that people of faith need to coexist peacefully.

I agree with Bono in that, but coexistence is not the same thing as conformity. This gives us a good reason to do a crash course in the four main world religions (excluding Christianity), just to acquaint ourselves with their many differences.

Here are some big points to keep in mind before we launch into each religion. You can divide the major world religions into two categories—*esoteric* and *exoteric*. Hinduism and Buddhism are the major religions of the East, and they are *esoteric* in nature, which means they focus on a type of mystical, spiritual enlightenment. They value spiritual experiences and technique over adherence to a book. Judaism, Christianity, and Islam are *exoteric* in nature, meaning they state that God has shown himself to us in an outward, historical way through revelation. You can also divide the major religions by their view of time. Western religions have a linear view of time—there was a beginning to this universe, and there will be an end. Eastern religions have a cyclical view of time, which means things are moving in a circle, which has no beginning and no end. The goal of many Western religions is to be accepted by God on that final day of judgment, whereas the goal of many Eastern religions is to escape the cycle of reincarnation.

Hinduism on the Whole

Okay, let's look more specifically at the religions of the East. Hinduism is the oldest religion in the world. It came on the scene somewhere around 1400 BC. It is probably the most difficult religion to understand and define because there was no founder. And it also has over 30 million gods. Hinduism is very mystical and is fully available to only the enlightened few.

Another striking characteristic of this religion is that you could go to one of its monasteries in India and you would find pictures of all the great religious leaders. You might find one of Muhammad, Jesus, Buddha, and so on. On Christmas day, Hindu monks will even bow down and worship Jesus Christ. They don't worship him exclusively, but they worship him as someone who represents the divine presence or who was a great sage or guru.

You…realize that *atman*—**your personal soul—is really at one with Brahma—the impersonal and universal force. This realization is what's known as** *nirvana.* **(No, it has nothing to do with the rock group.)**

In its nonspecific tendencies, Hinduism is a challenging religion to grasp. There are a multiplicity of forms and sects that tie into and stem from Hinduism. At its core, it is also pantheistic, so there is no real difference between the creator and the creation. Ultimately, all is one.

Here are some key terms in Hinduism:

- *Brahma* is the word Hindus use to describe the universal soul. Brahma is the impersonal absolute and is the closest thing to the single God in Christianity, Judaism, and Islam.

- *Karma.* Most likely you have used that term at one time or another. Maybe you have jokingly said, "Hey, I've got good karma today." (John Lennon wrote a song a long time ago called "Instant Karma's Gonna Get You.") Karma is basically the concept of reaping and sowing. See, in Hinduism, when you die you don't go to heaven or hell; instead, you have a rebirth. Again, that's the idea of reincarnation. So if you practice good deeds and build up good karma, then you will be reincarnated to a higher state. But if you have bad karma, then you will be reincarnated into a lower state, such as a rat.

- *Samsara* is the name for the wheel of karma, or the wheel of reincarnation. The goal of Hinduism is not to be forgiven of a personal sin. (How can you have a personal sin against an impersonal force?)

- *Moksha* is the goal of Hinduism, that is, to achieve release from the cycle of samsara.

Now, you can attain moksha in three ways:

1. *The way of knowledge,* which comes through listening to the sages and through reading scriptures (which come from a variety of sources; some of the main Hindu scriptures are the Bhagavad Gita, the Vedas, and the Upanishads). Then you would also turn inward to realize that *atman*—your personal soul—is really at one with Brahma—the impersonal and universal force. This realization is what's known as *nirvana.* (No, it has nothing to do with the rock group.)

2. *The way of devotion* is a more popular way. That is when you choose a particular deity to focus on and pray to, and through your devotion to that particular god, you will break through and achieve release from samsara. There are three major gods in the Hindu religion: Brahman, the Creator; Vishnu, the Preserver; and Shiva, the Destroyer. So someone who chooses the way of devotion may pick one of these three gods, or he may pick one of the incarnations of these gods (this is where a lot of Hindus' pantheism, or worship of nature, comes from), and he would devote his life to this

god and pray that through his devotion he would achieve release from the cycle of reincarnation.

3. *The way of works* is usually the way of monks in the Hindu faith. They achieve moksha through ceremonies and sacrifices and also through doing good deeds for other people without a desire to be praised or to be thanked.

Buddhism for the Unenlightened

Now, around 525 BC there was a Hindu who became disenchanted with some of the elements of his religion. He was particularly disturbed by the *caste system,* the rigid organization of social classes, that existed in traditional Hinduism. He began to wonder what ultimate reality, or truth, is and what the biggest problems in life really are.

This young Hindu's name was Siddhartha Gautama. He was reared in a very wealthy and influential home, and it was prophesied at his birth that he would either become the Prince of India or a monk. His family tried to protect him from seeing the outside world and all the misery and suffering that comes with it, but young Siddhartha escaped from the boundaries of home and saw four distressing signs—a sick man, an old man, a dying man and, lastly, a monk. These things greatly disturbed him and led him to the realization that birth, old age, sickness, and death come to everyone—not only once, but repeatedly.

Siddhartha decided to abandon his "worldly" life, leaving behind his wife, child, and rank, to take up the life of a wandering holy man in search of the answer to the problems and pains of life and death, life and death, and so on, in succession, since the beginning of time. He decided that he would become an ascetic monk, and for years he beat himself, starved himself, and tortured his body to try to understand the riddle of life. One day he started to meditate under what is now known as the bodhi tree. He stayed there for many days fasting and praying, until one day he walked out from underneath the tree, took a shower, put on some regular clothes, and said, "I am the Buddha. I am the Enlightened One." And so he left his asceticism and chose a middle path. From then on, Buddha gathered some disciples around him and began to teach them the Four Noble Truths.

So Buddhism was birthed out of Hinduism, and understandably, there are many Hindu concepts that carry over into this faith. Here are the Four Noble Truths that Buddha came up with:

1. Life is suffering.

2. Suffering is caused by a desire for pleasure and a desire for prosperity.

3. Suffering can be overcome by eliminating our craving for pleasure and prosperity.

4. We achieve this by following the Eightfold Path.

Now, the Eightfold Path has eight "right" steps:

1. *Right view:* to understand and acknowledge the Four Noble Truths of Buddhism.

2. *Right thought:* to have right motives in everything.

3. *Right speech:* to speak clearly, with truthfulness.

4. *Right action:* to do the right thing—respect life, earn what you have, control desires.

5. *Right living:* to have a profession that is an honorable one. For example, a Buddhist could not be a butcher because they do not believe in killing things.

6. *Right effort:* to continually strive to suppress our evil desires and cravings.

7. *Right mindfulness:* to be self-aware.

8. *Right meditation:* to practice the right yoga techniques and cultivate focus and concentration.

When you follow the Eightfold Path according to Siddhartha Gautama, the Buddha, you will experience nirvana (which you probably remember from Hinduism). Nirvana means *to extinguish*—literally, *to blow out*. So nirvana is achieved, basically, when you take away all your desire and all your craving for peace and prosperity.

To be a Buddhist, you don't necessarily have to believe in a god. Buddha, himself, never claimed to be god. He thought that miracles and the supernatural were merely distractions from the real goals in life—to eliminate pain and suffering.

Islam in Summary

Okay, let's move on to the religions of the West. We'll start with Islam, which is the second-largest religion in the entire world (Christianity being the first, but Islam is catching up). Islam is a very evangelistic religion, whereas Hinduism and Buddhism are much more passive. It is quickly growing around the world for a couple reasons. First of all, it uses force. Second, Islam is a very clear and rationalistic faith. You don't have to go through a lot of gymnastics and "experiences" to become a Muslim.

Islam was founded in AD 622 by Muhammad, so it came onto the scene about 600 years after Christianity. Muhammad was born in the city of Mecca, in Saudi Arabia. He married a very wealthy widow who was about 15 years older than he was, and when he was 40 he began to have visions. He didn't know if they were demonic or divine in origin. He asked his wife, and she said that she thought it was the angel Gabriel speaking to him. So over the course of his life, Muhammad wrote down these different visions, and that is where the Muslims get their holy book—the Koran.

Having been birthed out of Judaism and Christianity, Islam combines elements of both. For instance, Muslims accept the Genesis account of creation, and they acknowledge a judgment—a heaven and hell. They also believe in the virgin birth of Jesus Christ, but they see him as only a prophet, alongside Abraham, Noah, and Moses. Ultimately, however, Muslims believe that Muhammad is the main prophet of God and that the Koran is a scripture superior to the Bible. They have their own form of the Ten Commandments, in which they are told not to steal, not to lie, not to drink, and not to gamble. But most importantly, a true Muslim must adhere to the five pillars of Islam:

1. *The creed*—that is, the *shahada.* A Muslim must state publicly and passionately that there is no god but Allah and that his prophet is Muhammad. (Islam is a monotheistic religion. They believe in Allah, and the word *Islam* means, literally, to submit to the will of Allah.)

2. *Prayer.* Devout Muslims pray five times a day facing Mecca, the birthplace of Muhammad. (That is where you will find his tomb also.)

3. *Almsgiving.* Each Muslim is required to give one-fortieth of his income and estate to the mosque.

4. *Fasting.* If you follow basketball, you may know that NBA all-star Hakeem Olajuwon will fast during the month of February, which is presently the month of Ramadan on the Islamic calendar. He will refrain from eating or drinking from sunup to sundown.

5. *Pilgrimage.* If at all possible, at some point in their lives Muslims need to make a pilgrimage to Mecca and visit the tomb of Muhammad.

Depending on how well a Muslim upholds these five pillars, he or she will receive varying degrees of rewards or punishment in the afterlife.

Judaism in Short

Judaism is the foundational religion of both Christianity and Islam. It is a monotheistic religion, with one God, who is Creator, Ruler, and Judge of the World. The personal name of the God of the Jews is *Yahweh*—he is all-knowing, all-powerful, and everywhere-present. Abraham is the father of the Jews; David, their greatest king; and Moses, their most influential prophet.

Jews adhere to all 39 books of what Christians call the Old Testament. But unlike Christians, they do not hold the books to be equal in weight. The *Torah*, or the Books of the Law (the first five books in the Old Testament), are the most authoritative documents, and then the Prophets, and to a much lesser extent the *Writings* (the poetic books, history books, and what's know as the Five Scrolls).

God made the Jews his chosen people and promised Abraham possession of a certain piece of land and descendants that would outnumber the stars. The Jews are looking forward to the coming of Messiah, who will give them back their land and dominion on earth. They place a heavy emphasis on the Law of God and the keeping of the Sabbath. Repentance and obedience to the Law as revealed in the Torah and *Talmud*—a vast collection of Jewish laws and traditions—is the path to knowing God now and in the afterlife. There is a lot of common ground between Christians and Jews because of their shared beliefs in the inspiration of the Old Testament. For this reason, I have not gone into great detail on Judaism.

Also, bear in mind that there are many offshoots and sects within Judaism, just as there are in Hinduism, Buddhism, Islam, and Christianity. Giving an exhaustive account of them would require another book, or two...or ten.

HOW DO YOU HANDLE CONFLICT?

In a nutshell, if you say it doesn't matter what your religion is because they are all the same, you are seriously ignoring some blatant conflicts. Just to review a few, Christians teach that God is personal; Buddhists teach that god is impersonal. Muslims teach that there is only one god, Allah; Jews teach that there is only one God, but he most certainly is *not* Allah; Hindus teach that there are millions of gods. I could go on and on with the differences, but hopefully by now you're seeing it's impossible for all of these doctrines to be true at the same time.

Allow me to illustrate with an example. Say you're walking in the park and you catch up to a woman who is obviously pregnant, also out for a walk. You ask her, "When's the baby due?" She replies, "In just three more months." Now you happen to be walking at a pretty good clip, and you've lapped her. Just imagine that when you approach her again, you ask the exact same question ("When's the baby due?")—but this time she says, "I'm not pregnant, you jerk!" You say, "I just asked you the same question, and you said you were, so which is it? Are you pregnant or not?" She says, "Well, I'm both." I don't have to go into how ridiculous that would be. No one can be pregnant and not pregnant at the same time. By the same token, God cannot be personal and impersonal at the same time. Jesus cannot be *just* a "good teacher" and God in the flesh at the same time.

So how does a religious relativist deal with the conflicting truth claims among the world religions? It's as though he takes out a giant blender and throws them all into it. He takes the beliefs of the Jewish people, the Muslims, the Christians, the Buddhists, the Hindus, and whatever else he wants to add and presses *grind, blend,* or *puree,* obliterating their uniqueness. What results is the bland concoction that is relativism. Though they say they do, relativists don't truly listen to the voices of others. They would show more of the respect they profess by recognizing the opposing truth claims of the different world religions rather than conforming these religions to their own relativistic grid.

In essence, religious relativism offends where it sought to embrace. I once took part in a PBS interfaith dialogue with a Buddhist monk, a Jewish rabbi, and an Islamic layperson. As the discussion unfolded, we discovered we had some agreement in terms of morality, but we recognized we had radically different belief systems; in the end, we cordially agreed that we disagreed. I also have a good friend who is an Orthodox Jewish rabbi. I respect him greatly and have learned much about God and the Bible from him. We do agree on many things, but we have a strong disagreement when it comes to Jesus Christ.

Probably like you, I have friends from a variety of faith perspectives whom I enjoy talking with, debating, and challenging. It's important that we interact with people from different perspectives. But the "all paths" point of view tries to say we are all teaching the same thing—which we are not. Any true believer in Judaism, Buddhism, Islam, or Christianity knows that major differences exist between us. We are okay with that, but many religious relativists are not. If you are reading this and you consider yourself to be a religious relativist, please do not throw us into your blender. Do not do violence to that which we hold sacred. Let us disagree in peace. We can handle it, I assure you.

RELATIVISM IS A RELIGION

Not only does religious relativism offend where it sought to embrace, but it also ends up creating the very thing it is criticizing. While relativists are busy denouncing absolute truth claims, they are simply making their own. Relativism is "the way, the truth, and the life" to them, and they expect all the religions of the world to bow down and act in deference. They are just as dogmatic about all paths leading to God as someone who believes in just one way. They can be just as intolerant and just as judgmental too. You'll never find a *true* relativist who authentically embraces the various faiths of the world. Religious relativism is a distinct religion in and of itself.

Perhaps by now you're thinking, *Well, if religious relativism doesn't really pan out when you analyze it, and if all paths can't lead to God, then what is the correct path?* (You've probably already guessed where this is going, but hear me out.) Why the Christian path? What makes it different? Herein lies the distinction between the Christian path and all the rest: All the other paths are human attempts to get to God. Christianity is all about *God's* initiative. He built a bridge for us. We don't have to build it. And he didn't just build it, he also (through Christ) provided the means by which we cross it. It makes perfect sense when you really think about it. If God is in control and all-powerful, as most religions assert, wouldn't it follow that he would have to be the one to initiate the path? For the same reason, wouldn't it also follow that he would be the one enabling us to travel it?

So if this God who's in control of everything has taken the initiative and given us a way to connect with him and know him, it would have to be the height of arrogance for us as mere human beings to reject his path and try to come up with our own.

If you get down to the bottom of things, I would say it's not the exclusivity of this path that is the turnoff as much as the attitude with which it's presented. We'll talk more about attitudes that turn off in the next chapter.

QUESTIONS TO THINK OVER

1. Before reading this chapter, did you believe that all paths were equally valid routes to the same destination or God?

2. After having read the chapter, has your position changed? Why or why not?

3. Explain how relativism ends up creating the very thing it criticizes.

4. What distinguishes the Christian path from all the others?

Chapter 3

Because All Christians Are Hypocrites

• • • • • • • • • •

Seinfeld has to be one of the most brilliant comedies to appear on TV in decades. Now that it's in syndication, it's hard to flip through the channels without catching a glimpse of Jerry, George, Elaine, and Kramer. This show "about nothing" often revealed much of the human soul...even if by accident. One episode, called "The Burning," was particularly insightful. In it, Elaine's boyfriend, David Puddy, tells her she is going to hell (a place filled with ragged clothes) because she doesn't have a "Jesus fish" on the back of her car. Of course, the irony is—as is later pointed out by the priest—Puddy is supposed to be a Christian, and yet he is sleeping with Elaine out of wedlock.

THE JESUS FISH

Have you ever met a Puddy before? Maybe you've been cut off one too many times by a "Jesus fish" driver. Or maybe you've done business with a What Would Jesus Doer who was more like a What Would Judas Doer...and who ended up stabbing you in the back. Perhaps your biggest beef isn't with Christianity itself, but with Christians.

Mine too. See, I was born and raised in the church. My dad has been in church work for about 40 years now, my older brother has for 20, and I have for about 18. During these decades I've seen incredible levels of hypocrisy. I'm talking about Bible-toting-Scripture-quoting people who finally showed their true colors, and they weren't pretty. I've known hypocrites, believe me, and I hate hypocrisy as much as you do (maybe even more, given what I've seen).

Okay, that said, let's go over some facts about hypocrisy. Perhaps the biggest one we need to just lay out there is this: Mike was right...there *are* hypocrites in the church, and if you're turned off by them, you're in good company. Here are some things to check out.

Fact #1: Jesus Christ Hates Hypocrisy

When Jesus was on this earth, he was constantly at war with hypocrites. Take a look at his words as recorded by Matthew:

> Woe to you, teachers of the law and Pharisees, you hypocrites! You are like whitewashed tombs, which look beautiful on the outside but on the inside are full of dead men's bones and everything unclean. In the same way, on the outside you appear to people as righteous but on the inside you are full of hypocrisy and wickedness.[1]

Those are some pretty tough words, wouldn't you say? There's a lot more where that came from. Just read the rest of Matthew, along with Mark, Luke, and John, and you'll see that a huge chunk of the Gospels is devoted to Christ's many diatribes against hypocrisy, most of which were directed right at the main culprits of the day—the Pharisees. These holier-than-thou types thought their religiosity would put them in good standing with God.

Well, they couldn't have been more wrong. Granted, all of us fall short in our own efforts, but what was so unbearable about these prigs was their claim to such piety. Jesus gives a whole list in Matthew of ways in which they fell short of the Law they professed to hold so dear. He continually raged with a righteous anger against these men in order to wake them up from their hypocritical slumber. So, as I said earlier, if hypocrites make you angry, you are in *good* company—the very best, in fact.

Fact #2: Hypocrites Happen

Hypocrites happen in all sorts of places, not just in the church. It just so happens, though, that the church is where they seem the most offensive. In reality, we shouldn't be so shocked by their presence—we've received fair warning. Christ specifically said we would find them there and told us to be on our guard, saying there would be many wolves dressed in sheep's clothing. John, one of Christ's closest followers, also predicted that false teachers and hypocrites would infiltrate the church.

> **Only you truly know the damage that's been done inside you, and you know all too well that no human can make it right. It will take something from God.**

Paul mentioned them in his letters as well, encouraging those who were new in the faith to watch out for folks who appear to be harmless but are actually bent on wrongdoing. There have always been hypocrites and backstabbers in the church, and there always will be. You don't need a PhD in church history to know of some of the many atrocities committed by people who called themselves Christians. To name just a few: the Crusades, the Spanish Inquisition, the Salem witch trials, the various scandals of the 1980s involving famous (now infamous) televangelists, and the more recent—or more public, I should say—child molestation scandals with Catholic priests.

I know there are many people who have been hurt and abused by someone in a church setting or someone who called himself or herself a Christian. Perhaps I'm speaking directly to you. Maybe you were forced to do something you knew wasn't right or were made to jump through some religious hoop. Maybe you were embarrassed somehow.

Only you truly know the damage that's been done inside you, and you know all too well that no human can make it right. It will take something from God. I want you to know that he is willing and wanting to give that to you. And please just let me say this: As someone who has grown up in the church, as someone who is trying to follow Christ, I apologize. I'm sorry for the initial blow and the pain that followed. I'm sorry for the mistrust you now feel because of it. I want you to know that Jesus is on your side, that he will take care of you, and that he will also deal with the one who hurt you. In the meantime, he says we need to be on our guard.

LEONARDO AND THE GREEKS

Fact #3: "Sinner" Does Not Equal "Hypocrite"

One of the most crucial facts to see (along with Fact #1) is, there is a definite distinction between someone who is a hypocrite and someone who is just a sinner.

A *hypocrite* is someone who pretends to be something he is not. The word *hypocrite* comes from the Greek word *hypokrites,* which basically means "one who plays a part." You may have heard of the glory days of the Greek theater, when only one or two actors would perform an entire play. It didn't matter how many characters were in the play—these actors could pull it off because they had a variety of masks to wear. Well, these actors were called "hypocrites." Or perhaps you saw the movie *Catch Me if You Can* a few years ago. Leonardo DiCaprio's character is a hypocrite in the literal sense—he poses as a pilot for PanAm, as well as a medical doctor, and a lawyer. Jesus called the Pharisees hypocrites because their righteous façades did not match the state of their hearts and minds, which was of little importance to them.

A *sinner,* on the other hand, is someone who breaks God's law and falls short of his standard of perfection. One of the prerequisites for being a Christian is admitting that you are a "lawbreaker"—a sinner. It wouldn't make any sense for *sinner* and *hypocrite* to be the same thing, because no religion would have hypocrisy as a prerequisite. (If there *is* a church with this prerequisite, please tell me where it is so I can stay as far away from it as possible.) Paul, who wrote 13 books of the New Testament, called himself the "worst of sinners," yet he vehemently denounced hypocrisy. Remember, a hypocrite is someone who pretends to be someone he is not. Paul, obviously, did not fit this description. He recognized he was a sinner in need of God, as all of us are.

So what exactly is a Christian? A Christian is a sinner who is actively seeking to eradicate any duplicity present in his or her life. Allow me to explain: If you are a Christ-follower, then God accepts you on the terms of Christ's sacrifice and declares that you are right with him. You have been given a new, pure identity that is independent of anything you can do (or not do, even). Because this new identity is independent of your behavior, it is still possible for you to sin, and all Christians do every day—in thought, word, or deed. As a Christian, though, you own up to the sin inside of you and aspire to live up to your *true identity* in Christ by daily agreeing with him about your sin, by talking with him, by consulting and learning from his book, the Bible, and by trying to please him in all that you do. Therefore, we can easily conclude that all Christians are sinners, but not all Christians are necessarily hypocrites.

Now, I can't very well write a chapter about hypocrisy without talking about one of the biggest hypocrites I know of—me! I don't mean I'm a hypocrite in the pure sense of the word, but I certainly feel like one because I know I don't live up to everything I proclaim. I teach others to love their neighbor, to live in a giving way, and to talk to God often; however, I find myself being unloving to my neighbor, living in a self-focused way, and forgetting altogether to talk to God. Not only that, I also lose my cool, judge others for not being as spiritual as I often fancy myself to be, and fail to live out many of the messages I put forth. Yes, I am gifted at sinning. At the same time, though, I hate the duplicity I see in my own life, and I ask God to remove these defects in my character.

DO COUNTERFEITS NULLIFY THE GENUINE?

If you're still too turned off by hypocrites in the church to even consider Christianity, think about this question: Does the presence of counterfeits nullify the genuine? In other words, because there are hypocritical Christians in the church, can none be authentic or genuine?

Let's go back to Leonardo in *Catch Me If You Can* and see if he sheds light on the subject. Because his character was posing as a pilot for PanAm, does that mean there were no real, certified pilots in that airline? What about medical doctors? Since he pretended to be one but wasn't, does that mean all doctors are quacks and phonies? What if I showed you a counterfeit $50 bill? Would you turn down the one your grandfather gives you for Christmas because all $50 bills are suddenly counterfeit? Take Picasso prints. Do they nullify authentic Picasso paintings? Or take cubic zirconium. Because there are man-made diamonds, are there no genuine stones that come out of the ground anymore? Say you read an article on crooked cops. I bet you'll still call 9-1-1 if someone is breaking into your house.

Hopefully, you're getting my point. In fact, this argument simply turns in on itself when you press it because there has to be something authentic in order for there to be a counterfeit of it.[2]

So now we come to the real question: Is your claim that all Christians are hypocrites a genuine reason for your not accepting Christianity, or is it just an excuse? If you're honest, you'll admit it is more of an excuse than a genuine reason. I think there are a lot of people who use this argument, and many others like it, as part of a defense mechanism. It prevents them from having to deal with the real issue—which is not who and what Christians are, but who and what Jesus Christ is. Jesus Christ is not a hypocrite, and you'll be hard-pressed to find someone even in the atheist or agnostic camp who would deny that he walked what he talked.

QUESTIONS TO THINK OVER

1. In general, which of the following do you believe?

    a) All Christians are hypocrites.

    b) Most people are hypocrites.

    c) People who think all Christians are hypocrites are simply trying to cover up a deeper issue.

    d) Hypocrisy is not unique to Christianity.

Explain your answer.

2. Describe the difference between a *hypocrite* and a *sinner.*

3. If you believe that the church is full of hypocrites, is that belief based on a specific experience?

4. If so, have you perhaps held the entire church responsible for the actions of one or a few people who hurt you?

Chapter 4

Because Evolution Is True

* * * * * * * * *

Not too long ago I had the opportunity to talk with Lee Strobel, who is one of the leading Christian apologists of our day.* I asked him to tell me a little bit about his spiritual journey. He began by recounting some experiences he'd had in his high-school biology class. One experience in particular had affected him more than any other, and that was learning about Darwin and the theory of evolution. He remembered coming to the conclusion one day that if Darwin was right, then God was out of a job. After realizing in that moment that the two were irreconcilable, he trusted in Darwin and squelched any semblance of faith he'd had in God. From that point on, and through much of his adult life, he was an avowed atheist.

Another former atheist named Patrick Glynn had a very similar experience. Here's what he said about it:

> I embraced skepticism at an early age when I first learned of Darwin's theory of evolution in, of

---

* An *apologist* is someone who explains and defends a viewpoint, thesis, or belief system.

all places, Catholic grade school. It immediately occurred to me that either Darwin's theory was true or the creation story in the Book of Genesis was true. They could not both be true, and I stood up in class and told the poor nun as much. Thus began a long odyssey away from the devout religious belief and practice that had marked my childhood toward an increasingly secular and rationalistic outlook.[1]

Can you relate to these guys at all? Perhaps you began to connect the dots of evolution back in school, and your faith in a Creator (if you had faith to begin with) completely dissolved. Or maybe you do believe in God, but in your mind evolution does sound rational, and this bothers you. Perhaps you are scared to ask some of the questions you may have for fear of compromising your belief in God. Whatever your stance, this chapter is going to give you some good mental jerky to chew on and will challenge you to really examine what you say you believe.

WHAT IS EVOLUTION, ANYWAY?

First off, we need to define some terms and figure out what we mean when we are talking about *evolution*. There are all kinds of theories involving evolution. We'll start with two key terms: microevolution and macroevolution. *Microevolution* refers to change within a species. In other words, it explains why we have various breeds of dogs.

On the other hand, *macroevolution* refers to change from species to species—a bird becoming a cat becoming a dog becoming a horse becoming an ape becoming a human. The best-known theory of macroevolution is commonly called Darwinian evolution. In general, Darwinian evolutionists conclude there is no God, nor is there any kind of transcendent, supernatural, or spiritual realm in the universe. (Or, if there is, it is completely irrelevant to scientific observation.) Instead, we live in a closed system. All we have before us is matter and molecules in motion—or, as Carl Sagan put it in the introduction to his *Cosmos* series on TV, "The universe is all that is, or ever was, or ever will be." This is a completely naturalistic view.

The next theory I want to mention is known as *intelligent design* and is the most recent player on the field. Those who hold to this theory point to various complex biological structures, such as the eye and birds' wings, and say these could not possibly have developed by purely random mutations and instead necessitate a designer—though they do not specify who or what this designer is. Many of them propose that certain forms of microevolution provided the mechanism by which this intelligent designer created the various species. Some, though not all, champions of this theory also believe in *speciation* (the creation of more than one species out of a single species).[2] As noted above, though this intelligent designer is not specified as the God of the Bible, there are, in fact, many Christians who hold to this theory. Dr. Michael Behe is one of them. You can check out his book, *Darwin's Black Box,* to get a much better idea of what the intelligent design movement is all about.

Lately, there's been quite a buzz around creation, evolution, and intelligent design. Too often the debate is grossly oversimplified to "Christian vs. Atheist" or "Creation vs. Evolution." What follows are five views within Christianity regarding creation and evolution. (It must also be noted that even within these camps are many diverse subsets and divisions of thought.)

- *Young-earth creation theory.* As the name implies, supporters of this theory believe the earth to be around 6000 to 20,000 years old, as opposed to the 4.5 billion years old that most scientists calculate according to standard dating techniques. They believe that God, by his direct and immediate action, created the Earth and its inhabitants in six literal 24-hour days, totaling 144 hours. They arrive at the date of the Earth by using a literal interpretation of the Hebrew word for *day,* along with the consecutive genealogies given in Scripture.

- *Old-earth creation theory.* Adherents to this theory also believe that God, through his intentional and direct action, created the Earth and all forms of life. They do not, however, agree that the Earth is just 6000 to 20,000 years old for a variety of reasons, the main one being that they do not interpret the six days of creation as literal 24-hour days, but as long periods of time. The Hebrew word *yom,* translated "day" in Genesis, can and is also translated more generally in other parts of Scripture as a long period of time, which could be millions of years rather than 24-hour days.

- *Gap theory.* This old-earth viewpoint also places God as the direct and immediate creator of the Earth and life. However, its proponents often agree with the 24-hour literal days of young-earth theory but then point to potential "gaps" in time—millions of years—surrounding the creation account in Genesis chapter 1. The gaps indicated, particularly between verses 1 and 2, lend support to the idea of a much older Earth.

- *Theistic evolution.* Theistic evolutionists believe in both God and the scientific account of evolution, and within this camp are subsets that divide over God's degree of influence and participation in the process of evolution. Their main point is that there is a sovereign God who either allowed or intended for evolution, a natural process, to be the means by which all creation came into being. A person of this persuasion would view evolution as the natural progression of God's methods rather than a phenomenon precluding God's participation.

- *The framework hypothesis.* Those who adhere to this theory believe that the account in Genesis was not written as a scientific document with the intent and purpose of explaining the precise details of how and when creation came into being. Thus, it cannot be read as such. Rather, it should be read and interpreted within the context of its intention at the time of its writing (the time of Moses)—an era that, they believe, lacked even a scientific understanding, much less the language to express it.

IN DARWIN WE TRUST

My point in explaining these various theories to you is to show that believing in "evolution" doesn't necessarily cancel out believing in God. That said, I'd like to address macroevolution, or Darwinian evolution, because it is what's implicit in the title of this chapter—as well as whenever the average person is talking about "evolution."

What Charles Darwin basically theorized was that the cosmos, and everything we see in human beings and animals, are the results of three things: matter, random chance, and a whole lot of time. And since 1859, when Darwin published his magnum opus, *The Origin of Species,* this explanation has basically ruled the day in academia. And this theory's influence is not limited to fields of science. Darwin's ideas influenced Freud in a tremendous way, and therefore, psychology and sociology as we know them draw their lifeblood in many ways from Darwinian evolution.

So when you look at major intellectual and cultural influencers in the Western world—those in the grade schools, the universities, the graduate-level classes, many popular forms of media, as well as literature—you will find the vast majority of them buy into some type of Darwinian evolution. It's not the only story in town, but it's the only story that is allowed, and it's been very effective in its conquest of the "educated mind."

The bottom line here is that people have all sorts of agendas, and they'll use whatever means they can to rationalize their own lives and even sell their ideas to you.

One of the main reasons this theory has had such an influence on the whole of Western thought is because it draws such bold conclusions and then conceals them in scientific, "neutral" language. You'll see this quite often in the realm of metaphysics, which is simply the study of reality. Any topic, no matter how unrelated to science it may be, is free game—whether it's love, the existence of God, or simply a philosophical perspective. For example, take a look at the following quote by the late evolutionary biologist, Stephen Jay Gould:

> We are here because one odd group of fishes had a peculiar fin anatomy that could trans-form into legs for terrestrial creatures; because comets struck the earth and wiped out dinosaurs, thereby giving mammals a chance not otherwise available...because a small and tenuous species, arising in Africa a quarter of a million years ago, has managed, so far, to survive by hook and by crook. We may yearn for a "higher" answer—but none exists. This explanation, though superficially troubling, if not terrifying, is ultimately liberating and exhilarating.[3]

Did you catch that? Gould is spouting off a few scientific assumptions (mind you, even the scientific parts are *assumed* here) in order to bring home his own philosophical viewpoint. What viewpoint is that? Existentialism—plain and simple. He's saying that we merely exist to exist and that there's no real pur-pose. What's so "exhilarating" to him is the freedom he thinks his viewpoint guarantees. If there is no purpose or authority (aside from himself, of course), he's completely "liberated" to do as he pleases.

I'll give some similar but bolder quotes later on in the book, but the bottom line here is that people have all sorts of agendas, and they'll use whatever means they can to rationalize their own lives and even sell their ideas to you. Take movies, for example. Many filmmakers (actually it's more like "most") have an agenda. They have a particular worldview or life philosophy they are seeking to educate you about or persuade you to get in on. You can find this in almost any film, from a Disney cartoon to a David Fincher production. Now, they won't come out at the beginning of their movie and say, "The following movie is going to give you an overview of the philosophical viewpoint of nihilism, originated by Friedrich Nietzsche in Germany." They use the medium of cinema to communicate their particular worldview in a subtle—or sometimes not-so-subtle—way.

In much the same way, evolutionists can be sly in presenting what they have virtually no scientific basis for believing, much less teaching about, and they can get away with this because they mask their ideas in "scientific" jargon. This method seems to have worked for the last hundred years in spite of the major problems and weaknesses with Darwinian theory—but the holes in it are getting wider, deeper, and more and more exposed every day.

DISSENTING VOICES

It Doesn't Fit

I recently interviewed Dr. James Tour, a researcher in molecular electronics, chemical self-assembly, and many other areas.* In our chat, I asked him this question: "Dr. Tour, what are some of the problems you see with the theory of evolution?" Here is what he said:

> I have trouble with the Darwinian account because it doesn't fit; it doesn't fit the process in which molecular structure can change to build one entity and transform it

---

* Dr. Tour is currently the Chao Professor of Chemistry at Rice University's Department of Chemistry and Center for Nanoscale Science and Technology (CNST). He's done postdoctoral training at the University of Wisconsin, as well as at Stanford, and has also served as a visiting scholar at Harvard. In addition to those mentioned above, Dr. Tour's scientific research areas include conjugated oligomers, electroactive polymers, combinatorial routes to precise oligomers, polymeric sensors, flame-retarding polymer additives, carbon nanotube modification and composite formation, synthesis of molecular motors and nanotrucks, methods for retarding chemical terrorist attacks, and use of the NanoKids concept for K-12 education in nanoscale science. He has received numerous prestigious awards and has more than 250 publications with 20 patents or published patent applications.[4]

into another, into another, into another. I don't see the process for the life generation. We [scientists] don't even understand what goes on in a cell. We don't even understand the little machinery that goes on. People say, "Well, we can clone."...We do not understand what goes on in the nucleus of a cell to the degree that we need. We just can't understand it. The knowledge isn't there.

I can't build a machine. I don't even know how to understand life on that basis. I had a group of scientists sit in my living room in front of my kids (I wanted them to see this), and I said, "Take a cell. You have a cell. And that cell just died. No more life. Can you bring it back to life? Everything is there. Everything is in place. Everything is there." And they started arguing about this. "Well, what really is life?" "It's ionic potential," one person said. And the microbiologist said, "No, no, it's much deeper than that." And I said, "You guys can't even define life for me. You can't even bring that little cell back that has everything in place. It just died, and you are going to tell me that you understand a whole lot about this?" And they said, "No, we understand very little."

Maybe the high-school teacher understands a lot in their own mind, but when you really get to the details, you don't understand. I don't understand how we can have a theory, like Darwinian theory, and start to build such a grandiose scheme with so little knowledge.[5]

Unexplainable Systems

Not long after that I had the opportunity to talk with another dissenting voice—Dr. William Dembski, who is at the forefront of the intelligent-design movement. He is a mathematician, a philosopher, and an author.* Here is what he had to say about

---

* Dr. Dembski has taught at Northwestern and Notre Dame. He has done postdoctoral work in mathematics at MIT, in physics at the University of Chicago, and in computer science at Princeton University. He is a graduate of the University of Illinois at Chicago, where he earned a BA in psychology, an MS in statistics, and a PhD in philosophy. Dr. Dembski also received a doctorate in mathematics from the University of Chicago and, for fun, a master of divinity degree from Princeton Theological Seminary.[6]

the whole issue of Darwinism and some of the weaknesses he sees within the theory:

> If you really look at it...there are some classes of bio-
> logical problems, certain types of systems. A colleague of
> mine named Michael Behe calls them *irreducibly complex*
> systems. These are multipart, integrated systems where
> everything has to be in place for the basic function to be
> obtained. And these things have just resisted any sort of
> evolutionary, naturalistic explanation (you know, where
> there is no sort of design involved in them). And the
> interesting thing is, on the flip side, we *do* know how
> systems like that arise.
>
> What has become really the mascot of the intelligent-
> design movement is a little molecular motor on the backs
> of certain bacteria. They are called *bacterial flagella*. They
> are, basically, motor-driven, outboard, bidirectional pro-
> pellers, and they move the bacterium through its watery
> environment; and these things spin at 20,000 rpm and
> change direction in a quarter-turn. So they are spinning
> 20,000 rpm, and within a quarter-turn, they are spin-
> ning 20,000 rpm in the other direction. Howard Berg at
> Harvard will call this the most efficient machine in the
> universe. (He hasn't written this, but in public lectures
> he will call it that.)
>
> You look at this under an electron micrograph, and
> it's a machine. The biologists will call them molecular
> machines. And you've got a driveshaft, you've got the
> propeller part, you've got a hook joint, you have something
> that mounts this whole thing on its cell wall so you have
> disks. You've got stators, rotors—it's a machine.
>
> Now, how do you get something like that? Well, in
> our experience, there is only one way we know of how
> these come about, and that's by design.[7]

In talking with these men who work at the molecular level on a daily basis, the holes in the Darwinian theory become much more evident. However, you don't have to be a scientist and have a zillion PhDs to have some intelligent questions about evolution. For example, evolutionary theory cannot explain the mechanism of evolution. That's what both Dr. Tour and Dr. Dembski are getting at, though in different ways. It also cannot explain gaps in the fossil record that were there when Darwin published *Origin* in 1859 and have never been filled.

And evolutionists cannot explain the appearance of matter. Check out this quote from Dr. Hugh Ross, renowned Christian astrophysicist:

> Big bang cosmology...presents a problem for athe-istic scientists because it points directly to the existence of a transcendent Creator—a fact they dare not concede.[8]

When you think about it, logic tells us that someone or something has to be eternal—evolution cannot explain the eternality of matter. Evolution cannot explain how matter produced life. In other words, how could a nonliving thing—like the chair you're probably sitting on—produce a cricket? How did intelligence spring from non-intelligence? How did moral beings spring from something amoral? The truth is, evolution is just a *theory,* though it is falsely presented as fact most of the time. In order for something to be considered scientific fact, it has to be reproducible and testable; you can't reproduce and test evolution.

A Matter of Faith

In light of all these holes, it's puzzling to me how *religiously* the vast majority of scholars and academic types still cling to the theory of evolution. I mentioned my puzzlement to Dr. Tour, and this is how he responded:

> The number of people in academia that are really qualified to begin to think of some of these fundamental questions is a much smaller number. For example, there are social scientists that really are not experts in the science side,

but they will hold to [the Darwinian theory] quite strongly. They will hold to this because they think that *somebody* knows, but I just want to know that there *is* somebody [who can] explain to me how you get these sequences in these amino acids. That's the level in which I work.

I work at the molecular level. I spend years trying to put a particular organic moiety on a particular molecule, with a particular orientation, with a specific handedness, because all these molecules are generally chiral, meaning they have nonsuperimposable mirror images.

And we have tremendous trouble doing this when we can choose all sorts of solvent media, all sorts of temperature ranges, all sorts of metal-catalyzed reactions—whereas biological systems are restricted generally to aqueous media and, generally, to a small subset of elements that [biological systems have] available. "Explain to me how you are satisfied by this," [I would say], and to those who understand the level that I am getting at, the problem becomes far more difficult to rationalize.

Now, you may be having flashbacks to chemistry or biology class right about now, and you're starting to break out in hives. Don't worry—there will not be a pop test on nonsuperimposable mirror images at the end of this chapter.

FAITH VS. SCIENCE?

In the last 50 to 75 years, we have been led to believe a dichotomy exists between faith and science. In fact, most people in our mainstream culture would say you can't be a Christian and a scientist, because Christians are people of faith and scientists are people of fact. I very much respect the intellectual integrity of scientists like Dr. Tour and Dr. Dembski, who are willing to admit the limitations of their endeavors and of science.

For example, Dr. Tour was speaking of things on the molecular level that can't be proven (that don't have a mechanism to explain them) when I asked him this question: "Dr. Tour, are you telling me then that it actually takes faith to believe in evolution?" This is what he said:

> Certainly, certainly you are going to need a lot of faith to believe in evolution, to go from step A to step B. And those who say it's no problem for them, I think, are really rookies. They don't understand because they feel that, "Oh, well—scientists understand." No, scientists really don't understand; not at this level, they don't....They will look from a 30,000 foot level, and they say, "This changes into this changes into this." Well, that's a wonderful paradigm. Wonderful!
>
> But now let's get a little more detailed. How did that change occur? If I just even begin to push that a little bit, as I would in any other field of endeavor: "You put molecule A on the board, and you show me molecule B; what is the mechanism of that transformation?" I expect that of a student, to show that to me.
>
> If they are going to say, "This is what I started with; this is what I got," then I say, "Propose to me some mechanism by which that molecule changed, the discrete steps"—and if they can't, I have real trouble with their mechanism. I believe you have B. I believe you had A. But if you can't explain to me the mechanism based on something that begins to fit, that mechanism doesn't hold much water.[9]

Perhaps you are still saying you believe in the theory of evolution in spite of what Dr. Tour and Dr. Dembski say. You, obviously, have every right to believe what you want. However, please realize it takes just as much faith to believe in the theory of evolution as it does to believe in a God who created the universe and everything in it. In fact, according to Dr. Tour's and Dr. Dembski's perspectives, it takes a great deal more.

LEARNING FROM A FOUR-YEAR-OLD

Okay, let's come up for some air. I think we can learn a lot from my four-year-old daughter, Claire. She has learned a behavior that is pretty crafty and very practical for her. Whenever she gets in trouble for hitting her big sister or stealing her crayon, she will come to my wife or me in her own defense, crying, "It was an accident," with crocodile tears streaming down her face. But, on the other hand, when something happens to Claire—maybe her big sister steals her crayon or hits her—she comes running to us, saying, "She did it on purpose." (Something like this happened today, in fact.)

If I were to find a nice silver watch in the middle of the Swiss Alps, my absolute last guess would be that it was the product of random chance.

Now, you're probably wondering what in the world this has to do with our whole debate on the origins of life, but just hang with me. When you start whittling it all down, you'll see the debate actually has very little to do with evolution; it even has very little to do with whether the earth is six days old or six billion years old. When we look at the debate between those who believe in an intelligent designer (whether that intelligent designer is the God of Scripture or some other god or force) and those who believe in chance, you'll see that it was raging long before Darwin came on the scene in the 1800s and introduced the theory of evolution.

This brings me back to my four-year-old. Without realizing it, Claire reduced the whole argument into two simple components for me—one represents accident; the other represents purpose. One believes in a designer, while the other believes in chance. Now, the idea of a designer sounds the most logical to me. If I were to find a nice silver watch in the middle of the Swiss Alps, my absolute last guess would be that it was the product of random chance. No, I'd say, "Man, someone had to have designed this." And how much more complex is a snowflake, or your fingerprint, or the human eye, or a flower?

WHAT'S YOUR STARTING POINT?

Why do so many intelligent people (far more intelligent than I) disagree on this issue? How is it possible that Dr. Dembski and the famous Dr. Stephen Hawking could be looking through the same microscope, at the same molecule...and Dembski will see intelligent design, and Hawking will see random chance?

Ultimately, it all depends on your starting point. Your starting point, whatever it may be, will have a direct effect on the way you perceive data. If I am starting with a belief in a transcendent God and Creator, then everything—right down to the individual facts I perceive in the universe—will be viewed in light of this belief. By the same token, if I come from the perspective of philosophical naturalism, and I believe that we live in a closed system and that all we really have are molecules in motion, then, obviously, I'm going to interpret observations in a way that backs up my fundamental assumption.

Here's a practical illustration of the point I just made: Your view of your father plays a part in your view of God, for better or for worse (more on this in the book's conclusion, "Back to Barbecue"). Let's take it a bit further and point out, however, that your earthly father isn't God. In fact, he's nothing like him. My point? It is quite possible to be wrong in your original assumption.

We'll talk more about ultimate starting points at the end of the next chapter. In the meantime, I hope you'll seriously consider the different perspectives on the theories of evolution and the ideas of design that were presented here.

QUESTIONS TO THINK OVER

1. What is your position on evolution, creation, and intelligent design?

2. How does your answer to question 1 relate to your beliefs about the God of the Bible?

3. Do you separate people of faith from people of science? Why or why not?

4. Explain what nonsuperimposable mirror images are. (Just kidding.)

Chapter 5

Because the Bible
Is Full of Myths

• • • • • • • • • •

Stan hated Christians. One of his favorite pastimes was daring God to strike him with a lightning bolt right there in the cafeteria to prove his existence. He would then revel in rubbing the noses of his Christian onlookers in his "victory." Confronting, mocking—you name it, and Stan embodied it. He actually went so far one day as to burn pages of the Bible in front of a group of Christians just to get a rise out of them. On one hand, you probably have no desire to use the Bible as kindling, as my friend Stan did, but on the other hand, you may also have a number of reasons for rejecting the Bible as the true Word of God.

Perhaps you related to Mike's array of doubts about the credibility of the Bible. You may have found yourself in a similar conversation at one time, using what I call the 3M Approach: Myths, Miracles, and Monk-morphing.

NOT THE STUFF LEGENDS ARE MADE OF

First of all, if you were to say the Bible is full of myths, I would have to ask you what you mean by the word *myth*. If you have read the Bible and have studied classical literature at all, you have seen that the Bible is not written in a mythological style. Nor does it read like a fairy tale, which is highly fanciful. It reads like a record of history that contains a wide variety of literary genres—biography, poetry, narrative, and eyewitness accounts.

Let's take a moment to look more closely at one of these eyewitness accounts. See how realistic in nature John's account of the Pharisees and the adulteress is. These self-righteous men throw her at the feet of Jesus, testing him to see if he will condemn this "obvious sinner." Instead of condemning her, the writer reports that Jesus quietly begins writing in the sand. This is exactly what a true eyewitness would tell us—details he understood no more than we do. This is not the sort of detail that ends up in legends.

And what of the specific names and dates in the Gospel accounts that place them on an actual timeline? (For example, Luke mentions a census that took place "while Quirinius was governor of Syria.") These are not characteristic of the vagueness of legends either. Consider all the little insights into character we get, as well. Legends don't have such depth. If the Gospels are not genuine eyewitness accounts and are merely fantasy or legend, then not only did these Galilean commoners invent the biggest and most successful hoax in human history, but they also invented a unique and unprecedented literary form—the realistic fantasy—which is highly unlikely.[1]

Or here's a thought: Perhaps the reason people see the Bible as mythical is not because it has the characteristics of myth but because myth has the characteristics of the Bible. Consider the following story about Jack and Ron.

Jack was a very rational fellow who always used the dreadful technique of rhetorically tearing down philosophical arguments he didn't agree with. In spite of this highly rational bent, he was also a deeply imaginative man who regarded his creative and fantastical side as his most comfortable side. Even so, his rational side told him that while stories might serve to amuse, they did no good in teaching you about the things that really mattered. This last realization made him stifle what little he'd held on to of the Bible stories he'd heard as a child, and Christianity was relegated to childhood silliness.

Then one day he met Ron. What Ron did for Jack was to help him see that his two sides—his reason and his imagination—need not be in opposition with one another. And one night, during a walk through the beautiful grounds of Magdalen College at Oxford University, Ron showed Jack how the two sides could be reconciled in the Gospel narratives. See, the Gospels had all the qualities of a great human story, but they portrayed an actual event: God, the storyteller, entered his own story and became a human, ultimately bringing about a joyous conclusion from a tragic situation. Suddenly Jack could see that the warmth he had always felt from the great myths and fantasy stories was just a spark of that greatest, truest story, the story of the birth, life, death, and resurrection of Jesus Christ.

It was John Ronald Reuel Tolkien who helped Clive Staples Lewis harmonize his imagination and reason. And with the example of Tolkien's Silmarillion tales and The Lord of the Rings before him, Lewis learned how to communicate the Christian faith in imaginative writing. The results were The Chronicles of Narnia, the Space Trilogy, *The Great Divorce,* and *Till We Have Faces,* to name a few.[2]

DO YOU BELIEVE IN MIRACLES?

Most often, when people say they have a problem with the Bible because it seems mythical, what they are really saying is they have a problem with the supernatural—the parting of the Red Sea, the virgin birth, the walking on water, and the raising of the dead (just to name a few). This was definitely one of

Mike's reasons for rejecting the Bible as a reliable document. To quote: "The Bible is basically a bunch of myths...Miracles like that don't happen these days, and if they don't happen now, why would they have happened then?" In other words, "We now live in a modern, enlightened world, and everyone knows that miracles do not happen because they are contrary to the laws of nature." If you concur with Mike and reject the Bible because it contains miracles, let me ask a couple questions.

How do you know miracles do not happen today? Let's think about this question for just a moment. How much information would you really need to make such a claim? How much data about the natural realm would you have to have at your disposal to know for a fact that miracles are impossible? The answer is obvious if you're intellectually honest with yourself: You would have to know every conceivable fact of science to make the grandiose claim that a supernatural world does not exist.

How do you account for the immutable laws of nature, given your worldview? How do you know that nature operates in a law-like manner? Perhaps you would answer, "I know nature obeys certain laws because I can see and test those laws." The first problem with that answer is this: Not all of nature is contained in your minute experience. In philosophical argumentation, you are guilty of a *hasty generalization,* which means you are taking a tiny bit of evidence and universalizing it.

The second problem with your answer is a little more complicated: If all you can know is what you can see and test, then you really can know very little. Why? Because you cannot be sure the knowledge you take in at this present moment can be applied to the past or to the future. You may *assume* it applies, but you cannot *know*—because you can neither go back in time nor jump to the future to test it. This is one of the reasons atheistic philosopher David Hume said we cannot see causation (the relationship between causes and effects). In other words, you cannot determine that A necessarily causes B simply because B happens to follow A at a given point in time. You can see that B may follow A *most* of the time, but you cannot possibly know it always has or always will.

You can learn a lot about the difference between causation and mere correlation from Lisa Simpson in this humorous scene that appeared in an episode of *The Simpsons:*

Homer: Not a bear in sight. The "Bear Patrol" must be working like a charm!

Lisa: That's specious reasoning, Dad.

Homer: Thank you, dear.

Lisa: By your logic, I could claim that this rock keeps tigers away.

Homer: Oh, how does it work?

Lisa: It doesn't work.

Homer: Uh-huh.

Lisa: It's just a stupid rock. But I don't see any tigers around, do you?

Homer: Lisa, I want to buy your rock.[3]

If you cannot see causation, then you cannot say with any authority that there are certain laws nature has always obeyed and will always obey. Therefore, to reason that you can know miracles are impossible simply because Mother Nature follows certain rules is completely arbitrary, given your inability to account for these rules. The truth is, in order to do science or math, or even think and argue logically, you need an omniscient and omnipresent God who providentially controls and guides the universe in a predictable way.[4]

HAVE MONKS MORPHED THE TEXTS?

A common argument Mike used to cast doubt on the reliability of the Bible was that it had been "embellished" over the centuries. Maybe you agree with him and would say to me, "How can you be sure the Bible you have today is the original? Surely the scribes and monks who made copies of the original manuscripts changed the texts through the years, and therefore, no one can really know for sure if it contains the true words of Christ." Well, do you have evidence to back your claim? What if I said I didn't think Mark Twain really wrote *Huckleberry Finn* and accused him of plagiarizing the whole thing? I can make that argument all day long, but it is mere opinion if I don't provide you with evidence. Where is the evidence that medieval monks tampered with the original?

Furthermore, do you have any knowledge in the field of textual criticism? Here's what author and scholar Helmut Koester has to say on how the New Testament ("NT") does in that field:

> Classical authors are often represented by but one surviving manuscript; if there are half a dozen or more, one can speak of a rather advantageous situation for reconstructing the text. But there are nearly five thousand manuscripts of the NT in Greek.... The only surviving manuscripts of classical authors often come from the Middle Ages, but the manuscript tradition of the NT begins as early as the end of [the second century AD]; it is therefore separated by only a century or so from the time at which the autographs were written. Thus it seems that NT textual criticism possesses a base which is far more advantageous than that for the textual criticism of classical authors.[5]

Let's look at Plato as an example of the type of classical author Koester is talking about. Does anyone doubt that the words we read from *The Republic* are indeed Plato's words? Probably not. What about the history of the manuscript? Well, Plato wrote it in about 355 BC, and the earliest manuscript we have is from AD 900. That's a gap of more than 12 centuries, for those of you keeping score at home.

Now let's take the Scriptures, specifically the New Testament. It was written between AD 50 and AD 90, and the earliest manuscripts we have are from around the year AD 100. That's a gap of only 50 years. That's not a significant amount of time for tweaking of epic proportions—pun intended. (And what would have been the monks' motivation anyway?) Here's what even a liberal scholar like John A.T. Robinson has to say about the credibility of Scripture: "The wealth of manuscripts, and above all the narrow interval of time between the writing and the earliest extant copies, make it by far the best attested text of any ancient writing in the world."[6]

The New Testament and the Old Testament—check out the Dead Sea Scrolls if you want more evidence—are reliable books of antiquity. Their historical credibility is verified not only through stout manuscript evidence, but also through continuing archaeological discoveries that support the evidence for the lives of the people and the events mentioned in their pages.

Longevity and Reliability

And something must be said for the Bible's longevity. Look at what the *Times* of London has said about it:

> Forget modern British novelists and TV tie-ins, the Bible is the best-selling book every year. If sales of the Bible were included in best-seller lists, it would be a rare week when anything else would achieve a look-in. It is wonderful, weird…that in this godless age…this one book should go on selling, every month.[7]

Further, the Bible has been translated more times and into more languages than any other book. Highly unlikely stats for a book with sketchy credibility, wouldn't you say?

On top of all that, we could look at the Bible's amazing

influence on political figures, thinkers, writers, emperors…you name it. Here are just a few examples:[8]

- *Abraham Lincoln:* "I believe the Bible is the best gift God has ever given man. All the good from the Saviour of the world is communicated to us through this book."

- *George Washington:* "It is impossible to rightly govern the world without God and the Bible."

- *Napoléon:* "The Bible is no mere book, but a Living Creature, with a power that conquers all that oppose it."

- *Daniel Webster:* "If there is anything in my thoughts or style to commend, the credit is due to my parents for instilling in me an early love of the Scriptures.…If we abide by the principles taught in the Bible, our country will go on prospering and to prosper; but if we and our posterity neglect its instructions and authority, no man can tell how sudden a catastrophe may overwhelm us and bury all our glory in profound obscurity."

- *Thomas Carlyle:* "The Bible is the truest utterance that ever came by alphabetic letters from the soul of man, through which, as through a window divinely opened, all men can look into the stillness of eternity, and discern in glimpses their far distant, long forgotten home."

- *Thomas Huxley:* "The Bible has been the Magna Carta of the poor and oppressed. The human race is not in a position to dispense with it."

- *Immanuel Kant:* "The existence of the Bible, as a book for the people, is the greatest benefit which the human race has ever experienced. Every attempt to belittle it is a crime against humanity."

- *Charles Dickens:* "The New Testament is the very best book that ever was or ever will be known in the world."

- *Sir Isaac Newton:* "There are more sure marks of authenticity in the Bible than in any profane history."

Either all these people were duped—or there is, indeed, something powerful about this book.

THE BIBLE IS BAD PROPAGANDA

There is one last argument I would like to make for the credibility of the Bible. Some say that the Bible is nothing more than a piece of propaganda that's been used by political figures throughout history to further their own agendas.

A good piece of propaganda would not expose the faults of its so-called heroes, nor would it highlight the suffering of those faithful to it.

Here's why that line of reasoning does not work: The Bible makes a really bad piece of propaganda. The Scriptures are fraught with the many failures of its main characters and even heroes.

- We can start with Noah, who got drunk and passed out naked.

- There was Abraham, who lied about his wife being his sister on several occasions because he was afraid for his life.

- Moses was a murderer.

- David was an adulterer and a murderer.

- Solomon made pagan women his wives and lost his closeness with God.

- Judas—one of the original disciples—turned Jesus in for a meager 30 pieces of silver and then committed suicide.

- Peter denied Christ three times.

- Saul (later Paul) had followers of Jesus stoned to death while he looked on with approval.

And these are the guys who messed up. What about the innocent ones who were persecuted, sold into slavery, beaten, thrown to the lions, and even killed in some cases—like Abel, Joseph, Daniel, all the disciples...Jesus himself! A good piece of propaganda would not expose the faults of its so-called heroes, nor would it highlight the sufferings of those faithful to it.

Most Mormons are kind, salt-of-the-earth people, whom I respect in many ways, but one of their Scriptures, called Doctrines and Covenants, is an example of a great piece of propaganda. These scriptures glorify the words of Mormonism's prophet, Joseph Smith, while conveniently leaving out the fact that he was often persecuted and was hounded out of New York, Ohio, and Missouri. He was tarred and feathered, jailed, and accused of some serious crimes, too, but the Doctrine and Covenants doesn't divulge that information. It also doesn't say that 10 of Smith's 28 or so wives were already married to other men when he married them. Today, the Mormon church is America's fifth-largest denomination, with 12 million adherents worldwide and temples in 17 of the world's 50 largest cities. Not bad for a religion that began with only a handful of disciples in 1830.[9] Now that's good propaganda.

WHO IS YOUR ULTIMATE AUTHORITY?

All of us turn to an authoritative source for answers and information that will help us make sense of the world we live in. For the "world" of finance, many people turn to the *Wall Street Journal*. In the "world" of fashion, it is *Vogue* or *GQ* that is the authority. When it comes to ultimate issues, perhaps your standard is empiricism ("Seeing is believing") or rationalism ("I think, therefore, I am"). But whether you would define yourself as an empiricist or a rationalist, what you're ultimately saying is this: You are your own authority when it comes to deciding life's truths. As a Christian, I turn to the Bible as my authoritative source for answers about life.

As I write this, I can already hear your concern: "But why do you accept the Bible as the only divinely inspired book? Why not accept the Koran or the Bhagavad Gita as well?" My response is twofold.

1. The Bible is uniquely inspired and, as such, presents a unique worldview. It claims to be God's very words, and it instructs us that other sources that contradict or distort these words are to be dismissed. This does not mean I cannot find some truth in Buddhism, Hinduism, or Islam. However, ultimate truth is found in God's once-and-for-all revelation to mankind: the Bible. I have yet to find a more complete, authoritative source for life and all of its complexity.

2. Jesus is my ultimate authority. He claimed to be God revealed in a person, so his words are more authoritative than those of any other religious leader. My belief in the authority of the Bible stems from my faith commitment to Jesus Christ also, who regarded the Scriptures as authoritative and commissioned his followers to pass on his message to all people, in all places.

So, everyone has a standard to which he or she turns in order to make sense of reality. My standard is the revelation of God, who has no other need for verification. (That's what makes God *God*.) If there is a God who stands outside of temporal reality, then he has the ultimate interpretation on every fact in the known world and beyond. This does not mean that I, or any other Christian, have "all the answers," but it does mean we have placed our trust in Someone who does.

You may say this is a cop-out. But you can't avoid trust—it's a given everywhere around us and in everything we do. We are all believers—it's just a matter of who or what we choose to believe in. You may have noticed that throughout this book, I've refrained from using the terms *believers* and *unbelievers* to refer to Christians and non-Christians. Why? Because "doing so would encourage the totally erroneous notion that 'believing' or 'having faith' is something only some of us do," explains Michael Guillen, former ABC News Science Correspondent and theoretical physicist. "Truth is, every one of us 'believes.' Every one of us 'has faith.' What divides us are the different objects of our faith, our different gods."[10]

So suppose for a moment there is a God who rules everything and is the Creator—the Eternal, the All-powerful, and the All-knowing. Could you think of any higher authority than this God? What kind of God would he be if he needed a mere man or a mere man's philosophy to vouch for him? He certainly wouldn't be very "God-like," would he? Therefore, wouldn't you expect this God to speak with self-attesting authority? Who else could authenticate his revelation to humans? How could any person know what this God would say and be like in order to confirm this revelation?

Really it comes down to this: If you will not accept the Bible on its own terms, then what you are saying is that you will never accept a revelation from God. Only God, if he is God, could reveal himself with final authority, and that is exactly what he does. So those who reject the Bible reject it not for reasons of hard evidence, but simply because they have a different absolute measure by which they judge truth. I presuppose the Bible as my ultimate authority and foundation for truth, whereas they presuppose their own minds.

Let's take a breather and get simpler for a moment. Questioning the authority or authenticity of the Bible is, for me, a little like deconstructing "Mary Had a Little Lamb." Think about it. We could all hone in on particular aspects and pose our questions. For example, how little was the lamb exactly? Was it really little or just little in comparison to Mary? Perhaps

Mary is rather large. Or, did the lamb really follow her *everywhere* she would go? If it did, then why does the rhyme specifically say it followed her to school one day? Perhaps we must not take "everywhere that she would go" literally.

And on and on it goes, but no matter where our questions take us, we're still left with some undeniable facts: Mary did have a lamb. Its fleece was white. And it did go with her to school.

By the same token, no matter how much you want to deconstruct and question the Scriptures, you are still left with some unavoidable facts: There was a woman named Mary. She had a son named Jesus. He had many followers who wrote about him and who spread his claim that he was the Son of God. He was referred to as the "Lamb of God." And he changed the course of human history.[11]

QUESTIONS TO THINK OVER

1. Before reading this chapter, did you believe the Bible was

   a) the inspired, infallible word of God?

   b) simply a collection of good principles to live by?

   c) merely legend passed down through the years?

   d) good fire starter?

   Explain your answer.

2. After having read the chapter, have you changed your position? Why or why not?

3. Do you believe in the supernatural? Explain why or why not.

Chapter 6

Because of Evil and Suffering

• • • • • • • • •

This morning I turned on my computer and went to a news Web site to find out what's going on in our country and around the world, and the first thing I saw was that a roadside bomb had killed 10 and wounded 11 Marines near Fallujah, Iraq, in the deadliest attack in months. I scrolled down a bit more to see that two bodies discovered in Ohio, possibly those of two New Hampshire children whose father had confessed to killing and burying them somewhere along a 700-mile stretch of the Interstate in the Midwest two-and-a-half years previously. A little further down, I read that a man had been given the death penalty for kidnapping, raping, and murdering an 11-year-old girl.

WHERE WAS GOD ON SEPTEMBER 11?

We cannot read the news today, much less watch it, without being bombarded by murder, rape, and tragedy. This is one of Mike's biggest problems with Christianity. "Where was God on

September 11?" he demanded. In other words, where is God when evil and suffering strike? Or even closer to home, where is God in personal pain and struggles?

These are hard questions. To be honest, I don't think any human being knows how to answer them fully. And the purpose of this chapter is certainly not to attempt to give The Answer to our universal dilemma. Instead, we're going to look at it through a philosophical lens. We'll focus on determining whether or not the existence of evil and suffering is a logical reason for not believing in God as he is presented in the Bible and by the Christian faith.

Caveat established, let's get back to Mike. His argument is not a new one. David Hume, the eighteenth-century Scottish philosopher (whom you may remember from the previous chapter), placed this challenge: "Is God willing to prevent evil, but not able, then he is impotent. Is he able, but not willing, then he is malevolent. Is he both able and willing, whence then is evil?"[1] In other words, if God knows about evil but cannot prevent it, then he is not all-powerful. And if God knows about evil and can prevent it, yet he does not, then he is not all-good. If he is both of these things—all-powerful and all-good—as the Bible attests, then why is there evil and suffering? The only logical conclusion to many, including Mike, is that there must be no God.

But what he fails to understand, and Josh failed to articulate, is that we need God to even make an argument to deny the existence of God. Does this sound confusing? Okay, let's take a few steps back and dissect that statement.

If someone who says he doesn't believe in God were to come to me outraged by some injustice, I would ask him why he's so upset. If a person does not believe in God, then where does he get his standard for right and wrong? (Sound familiar? If not, read chapter 1 again.) He can say, "I don't prefer that," or "I don't like that," or "That was not pleasant," but he cannot say something is right or wrong—because to say that is to say he believes in a transcendent moral being who has communicated its ethics and its truths to everyone in every place. Greg Bahnsen puts it this way:

> Unbelievers will be required to appeal to the very thing against which they argue—a divine, transcendent sense of ethics, in order for their argument to be warranted.[2]

Here's a simple analogy to show Bahnsen's point: If my five-year-old daughter wants to slap me in the face, she has to get up in my lap to do it. Much in the same way, for atheists to argue the problem of evil and suffering, they have to borrow from the Christian worldview and absolute standard of right and wrong to even make their case. As the great Christian philosopher Cornelius Van Til simply put it, "Atheism presupposes Theism."

Ravi Zacharias articulated this same idea in his book *Can Man Live Without God?* In it, he retells a conversation with a student at the Harvard Veritas Forum on this same subject:

> As soon as I finished one of my lectures, [the student] shot up from his seat and blurted out rather angrily, "There is too much evil in this world; therefore, there cannot be a God." I asked him to remain standing and answer a few questions for me. I said, "If there is such a thing as evil, aren't you assuming there is such a thing as good?"
>
> He paused, reflected, and said, "I guess so." "If there is such a thing as good," I countered, "you must affirm a moral law on the basis of which to differentiate between good and evil....When you say there is evil, aren't you admitting there is good? When you accept the existence of goodness, you must affirm a moral law on the basis of which to differentiate between good and evil. But when you admit to a moral law, you must posit a moral lawgiver. That, however, is who you are trying to

> disprove and not prove. For if there is no moral
> lawgiver, there is no moral law. If there is no moral
> law, there is no good. If there is no good, there is
> no evil. What, then, is your question?"
>
>   There was a conspicuous pause that was broken
> when he said rather sheepishly, "What, then, am
> I asking you?" There's the rub, I might add.[3]

The logic is clear: Without the ultimate moral lawgiver, the argument of evil and suffering has no foundation.

GOD IS GREAT, GOD IS GOOD?

Now, if someone admits the existence of God yet insists, based on all the evil and suffering he sees around him, this God must not be "all good," I'd have to give him what author Gregory Koukl calls a "60-second response" and ask something like, "Well, do you think we should pass a law banning abortion?" Chances are this person will say, "No, we need to have the freedom to choose...even if I personally see it as the wrong choice, it should be up to the individual to choose what is right or wrong for herself." "All right—isn't the ability to choose between right and wrong necessary in order to have free will?" "Well, yes," he will most likely say. Then I would say, "So if God made us and said, 'I'm giving you free will, but your only choice is to believe in me and obey me,' is that really *free will?*" Is that freedom to choose? It can't be. It's kind of like the election in Iraq when Saddam Hussein was running for president against no one. If that's a real election, I'm Santa Claus.

> **If God took away our ability to choose, nothing
> we did would have any real meaning or impact.
> We'd merely be puppets. I don't know what you
> think, but to me, that's no way to live.**

It boils down to the fact that in order for us to have the free will we hold so dear, we must have the freedom to make our own choices—for better or for worse. And if we choose the "worse" over the "better," that doesn't mean God isn't good. In fact, isn't it *more* loving and *more* good of him to give us the freedom to choose? What is love if it's forced? Furthermore, if God took away our ability to choose, nothing we did would have any real meaning or impact. We'd merely be puppets. I don't know what you think, but to me, that's no way to live.

Now these are just two ways I might respond to someone who uses the presence of evil and suffering as a reason not to believe in God or to deny his goodness. But in reality, these are inferior arguments. The best argument is found in the Bible. Mike criticizes Josh for using the Bible so much in their discussion. Granted, Josh didn't present his arguments in the most effective way; however, if Josh sees the Bible as the foundation for all truth, how can he not use it in a discussion on such ultimate issues?

Literally, for thousands and thousands of years, people have been batting around the problem of evil and suffering. Every world religion tries to account for it in some way, and some of them, like Buddhism, are based solely upon the quest to solve the riddle that evil and suffering present. But, again, we are looking primarily from a Christian point of view here, since that is the belief system Mike has called into question. So if you're a skeptic, I'd like to ask you to indulge me a little here. Suspend your disbelief for just a moment, and approach the following paragraphs as if the Bible really is true. It may seem funny at first—but if you're secure in your disbelief, then you'll be perfectly comfortable with this exercise.

LET'S GET BIBLICAL

The Bible talks time and time again about evil and suffering. The oldest book in the Bible, the book of Job, faces it head on. And, if you know your history, you know that the whole New Testament—all the Gospels and all the letters (epistles)—was written during a time of intense suffering and persecution for all Christians, as well as those specific ones who were called by God to pen his Word. Or consider the symbol of the Christian faith; it's not a peace sign, a bong, or a Prozac logo. It's a cross—an instrument of torture and death. So at the very heart of the Christian faith, there is the issue of pain, evil, and suffering.

Thus far, we've been looking at this issue from a philosophical viewpoint, but given the context in which much of the Bible was written, it would only be logical to at least look at what it has to say about God and the problem of evil and suffering. We can begin like this:

1. The Bible teaches that God is all-powerful.
2. The Bible teaches that God is all-good.
3. The Bible teaches that evil exists.

How does evil exist? Well, with minimum searching through the Scriptures, we find evidence that God created angelic beings with some type of free will. We can also find where Lucifer (or Satan), along with many other angels, rebelled against God and was thrown out of heaven. Satan then lured Adam and Eve into rebellion, they blew it, and now we blow it every day. Evil is real. Satan, or the devil, is definitely real. We experience suffering on a personal level because of evil in the world, and we see others suffer as well.

Now, if we look at the above three premises by themselves—that God is all-powerful, all-good, and that evil exists—then, yes, Christianity has a very apparent and logical problem. But Hume and others like him are leaving out a fourth and very important point if they're going to remain consistent and biblically accurate. When we add this statement, it logically removes the tension in the so-called dilemma. And that's as follows:

4. God ultimately has a morally sufficient reason for the evil that exists.

This may sound like a cop-out at first, but let's take a look at the lives of some actual biblical figures and see if it pans out.

Abraham is a great one to start with. God tested Abraham's trust in and dedication to him by asking him to sacrifice his son Isaac. Abraham must have gone through some immense inner turmoil and pain upon this request, climaxing at the point where he lifted the blade. Here is his son, whom God had promised to him years before, and through whom God had said he would change the entire world for the better. And now this same God is asking him to offer this precious son as a sacrifice—to give him up after he'd waited so long for him! Abraham could have thought all kinds of things about God at this point. He could have thought God was erratic, unfaithful to his children and to his promises, or just plain cruel. But he didn't think these things. Check out what the book of Hebrews reports:

> By faith Abraham, when God tested him, offered Isaac as a sacrifice. He who had received the promises was about to sacrifice his one and only son, even though God had said to him, "It is through Isaac that your offspring will be reckoned." Abraham reasoned that God could raise the dead, and figuratively speaking, he did receive Isaac back from death.[4]

Abraham trusted both in what God had promised and in what he would provide, as well as in his goodness. And God rewarded him by pronouncing him right before him (God)*—and using him as an example for the rest of the world to follow. He also favored Abraham in a way many may not realize—he gave

---

* Christians have traditionally used the word *righteous* to describe the quality of having right standing before God.

Abraham insight into his very own heart by allowing him to understand the pain and anguish he himself would go through in giving up his one and only son, Jesus Christ. Nothing brings hearts and souls closer than hardship. Do you see the wonderful gift in that? Abraham would have a closeness with God that very, very few others would. He would have an understanding of God's heart that few others could fathom. It's no wonder he was called "God's friend," a phrase no one else in all of Scripture was honored with.

Job has to be mentioned if we're talking about testing. He was a man who had everything and who recognized God as the source of all that is good. Satan came along and questioned Job's dedication to God, saying Job would surely curse God if the good things and circumstances ceased to be there.

God gives us a unique perspective in this book, and we see how he actually gives Satan permission to take things away from Job and hurt him. As a result, Job lost everything in one day—his family, his business, his wealth, his health, and the respect of his wife and close friends. He lost every single thing that would bring him pleasure, comfort, and happiness in life. What happened to Job was nothing short of evil, but God had a morally sufficient reason for allowing it to happen. Job's faith and trust in God were steadfast in spite of his horrific circumstances, and God ended up giving him twice as much as he had had before. In all this, through immense pain and suffering, Job had the opportunity to show his dedication to God. In other words, his love was proven real, and Satan was proven wrong.

Jesus Christ's crucifixion—the greatest crime in human history. Was it evil? Yes. Were the intentions of those who beat him, spit on him, jeered at him, and ultimately nailed him to the cross, evil? Absolutely. But God had a morally sufficient reason for not only allowing this to happen but also planning it out. Jesus Christ, the innocent one, was brutally murdered for the wrongdoers. Talk about the ultimate injustice! God endured the pain of seeing his one and only son die—worst of all, he endured the separation from that precious son when all our wrongs were heaped on him.

What was God's reason for this? What could possibly have compelled him to put himself through something like this? Only he knows. In him is a desire to save us and shower his goodness, love, and mercy on us, a desire whose depth we'll never fully understand. (This is the concept of grace.) It seems we'd have to be God to completely understand it. "The secret things belong to the LORD our God."[5] He has revealed to us everything we need to know at this point. (That's a jagged little pill for those who feel they have to understand everything.)

Job reprised. Many of us will decide one day that we fully understand the problem of evil, of pain, of suffering, of injustice, and we'll declare what we've decided with all our might.* But if we go back to the book of Job we'll see that when he cries out to God in agony and asks him to come down from heaven and make sense of it all, God just answers him with a lesson in cosmology: "Where were you, Job, when I put the stars in heaven? Where were you, Job, when I separated this from this? Where were you when I made this planet? Where were you when I made this beast? Who are you, Job, to talk back to me?"[6] Pretty harsh, huh? But that's the way Scripture many times speaks when people confront God on this issue.

However, what's most striking to me is this: When Job cried out for an answer to all of the pain and suffering and misery in his life and God showed up and just asked Job a zillion questions

---

* Typically, people will fall into the "free-will" camp or the "predetermined" camp. The first group says that all the evil and suffering in the world is simply the consequence of decisions we make. The second group says that God or "fate" is in control, and that all the evil and suffering we see is caused by a greater power—either for that power's specific purposes, or for no reason we can determine.

    I believe there's truth in both arguments, but you'll end up on a slippery slope if you try to tie your faith too firmly to just one of them. By the way, if you're having trouble grasping these ideas, go rent the movies *Signs* and *Minority Report*. They present the tensions between these sides in very creative and entertaining ways.

of his own, *Job left satisfied*. That's what's amazing. That God simply showed up and said, "Hey, listen...I am God. I am what I am, I do what I please," somehow, someway satisfied Job.

THE RUDY REALIZATION

Basically, after you search and search for an answer to the question of evil and suffering, you are left with the "Rudy realization." If you saw the movie *Rudy*, the title character is trying desperately to get into Notre Dame. He wants it so badly he can taste it. One day he asks his priest something like, "Father, do you think I'm going to get into Notre Dame?" The priest wisely answered, "Listen, I've been following God for many, many years, and I've learned two things: There is a God, and I'm not Him." Many times when people press and press, it's as if God shows up and says, "Hey, you! Get off my cloud!"

No matter what, when we're faced with this issue from an intellectual standpoint, we're left with mystery. We're left with faith. Job got on his face and worshiped. What will I bow down to? What will you? It all goes back to your standard for truth or reality. Do I see God and his revelation as ultimate reality, or do I see my own interpretation as the standard? In other words, am I going to trust God's understanding of the events in my life and throughout the history of the world, or am I going to trust my own take on those events? Is my faith in God or in myself? Taking a leap is inevitable—it's a matter of where we leap to.

Everyone wrestles with the problem of evil and suffering. There are entire religions founded upon it, as we saw in chapter 2. To me, that's just further evidence there is a God. The fact we are all looking for the answer reveals our belief that there really *is* an answer. And if there is an answer that none of us can see, there must be some higher and infinitely wiser power out there who can see it.

But I guess it's all in your perspective. Bertrand Russell, Nobel Prize winner and famous atheist from Britain, declared, "No one can sit at the bedside of a dying child and still believe in God."[7] I would say the opposite. How could I sit at the bedside of a dying child and *not* believe in God? If you're Bertrand Russell, if you're an atheist, what are you going to say to the dying child? "Cheer up. You're just molecules in motion anyway; you're just going to become fertilizer in the cemetery"? To believe something like that goes against everything in us.

Where Is God for Me?

So far, we've been looking at this dilemma in a detached and philosophical way. Okay, let's reattach for a moment. Remember Lisa Beamer? Her husband, Todd, was killed in the plane that crashed in Pennsylvania on September 11. He was one of the heroes who said, "Let's roll," and most likely helped divert the course of the plane in an effort to save others' lives. Here's what Lisa, mother of two toddlers, with another child on the way at that time, said in retrospect:

> God knew the terrible choices the terrorists would make and that Todd Beamer would die as a result. He knew my children would be left without a father and me without a husband. Yet, in his sovereignty and in his perspective on the big picture, he knew it was better to allow the events to unfold as they did rather than redirect Todd's plans to avoid death. I can't see all the reasons he might have allowed this when I know he could have stopped it. I don't like how his plan looks from my perspective right now. But knowing that he loves me and can see the world from start to finish helps me say it's okay.[8]

"*It's okay,*" she said. I'm not even close to understanding or relating to the degree of pain Lisa went through. Wouldn't it be nice to have a God who did understand, relate to, and even feel our pain—the pain of rejection, of betrayal, of abandonment, of abuse, of separation from those we love, or of watching those we love hurt? What if we had a God who would get down to our level and see what it's really like to walk in our skin?

You know—God thought this was a good idea too.

QUESTIONS TO THINK OVER

1. If you believe in God, do you believe he is good? Why or why not?

2. Can true love exist in the absence of free will? Explain your answer.

3. Think back to a tough time in your life. Can you point to any good that came out of that experience? In other words, has it made you stronger or more compassionate or more faithful, or more determined to be a better parent or spouse, and so on?

4. Explain the concept, "Atheism presupposes Theism."

Chapter 7

Because Jesus
Was Just a Good Man

* * * * * * * * * *

Perhaps you have seen the movie *The Da Vinci Code,* starring Tom Hanks and directed by Ron Howard. I read Dan Brown's novel when it came out and really enjoyed it—it's quite a page-turner. Brown is an imaginative storyteller who weaves historical fact and fiction together almost as well as some of our politicians (sorry, couldn't resist).

But what may not be apparent to many who read the novel or saw the movie is that he is not a scholar when it comes to ancient literature, especially the Bible. His account of how the Bible was put together by the pagan Roman emperor Constantine in an effort to cover up the greatest secret in human history—that Jesus was married to Mary Magdalene and had a child with her, starting an actual dynasty that is still in existence in Europe—is so far-fetched it should be placed in the genre of fantasy.

If you haven't read it, let me give you a snapshot of what

the book says about the nature and identity of Jesus Christ. Brown writes that, at the Council of Nicaea in AD 325,

> Many aspects of Christianity were debated and voted upon—the day of Easter, the role of bishops, the administration of sacraments, and, of course, the *divinity* of Jesus...Until *that* moment in history, Jesus was viewed by His followers as a mortal prophet...Jesus' establishment as "the Son of God" was officially proposed and voted on by the Council of Nicaea...a relatively close vote at that.[1]

Brown continues on the next page,

> From this sprang the most profound moment in Christian history...Constantine commissioned and financed a new Bible, which omitted those gospels that spoke of Christ's *human* traits and embellished those gospels that made Him god-like. The earlier gospels were outlawed, gathered up, and burned.[2]

If that's not enough to make you want to go out and buy the book or see the movie, I don't know what would be. Think about it. What is the most foundational and at the same time staggering claim of Christianity? That Jesus of Nazareth was God wrapped in human flesh. Of course anything that calls that into question is going to have an audience. Couple it with a captivating story and fast-moving writing, and you'll have folks going on a quest for the "Sacred Feminine" faster than they learned Klingon (yes, there is actually a Klingon Language Institute; it is a legitimate nonprofit corporation).

Now to me, the mere fact that *The Da Vinci Code* has caused such a ruckus is proof the gospel *is* true, but I'm getting ahead of myself now. Let's go back to the question at hand—that being, just who was/is Jesus?

TO BE GOD OR NOT TO BE GOD: THAT IS THE QUESTION

For centuries, men and women, boys and girls, students and professors have asked this question over and over again. It is The Question. Throw out the evolution debate, the hypocrisy beef, and the challenges of relativism; when you skin it down to bare bones, it always comes back to the question of Jesus Christ's identity. He himself asked his followers the very same question: "Who do you say I am?"[3] Perhaps that is the question you're dealing with. Maybe you are like Mike and would say, "Yeah, Jesus was a good man, a great moral teacher—but God in the flesh? I just can't buy that."

Laying aside the easily debunked theories that Jesus never existed or that he was an alien from outer space or something like that, let's take a serious look at our options. There are many ways people respond to this question of Christ's divinity. Following are the five most popular takes.

1. Jesus never claimed to be God. If this is true and he indeed never called himself God, then where did such an outlandish idea come from? Some say his disciples made it up. After all, they had bought so heavily into his teachings that they had literally left everything to follow him. Making him God was their way of "saving face," if you will, as well as getting their upstart religion off the ground. They gave him an extreme makeover, adding a little here and taking out a little there, and the result was a supernatural facelift that would be utterly convincing and never lose its effects (not even today...pretty good surgeons, if you ask me).

Still others argue that neither Jesus nor his disciples ever claimed he was God—but that, as the New Testament was being written, scribes added a "mythic layer" on top of the Scriptures to make Jesus appear more Godlike (remember "monk-morphing"?). And then there are the conspiracy-theory types who actually claim the emperor Constantine made up and forced the idea of the divinity of Christ onto the early church leaders in AD 325 for the political purpose of unifying the Roman Empire. For the record, history shows that the emperor did in fact use elements of Christianity to unite his empire. However it does not show, by any stretch of the imagination, that Christ's deity was Constantine's own invention.

2. Jesus claimed to be God in a New-Age way. This option doesn't deny that Jesus claimed to be God but simply redefines what he meant by that claim. Many who fall into this camp make Jesus out to be an enlightened sage. Like Buddha, Krishna, Muhammad, and other great mystic leaders, Jesus taught the way to inner peace and happiness. When he made claims to divinity, he was simply trying to take us to a higher level of spiritual awareness by showing that we all have the spark of divinity inside of us. Sure, Jesus is god—just like Muhammad is god, Buddha is god, Krishna is god, and you and I are god.

For instance, I heard Deepak Chopra declare the following in a Larry King interview: "I don't think Christ was a Christian, I don't think Buddha was a Buddhist, and I don't think that Muhammad was a Muhammadan." On one hand, I would have to agree—Christ, Buddha, and Muhammad founded these religions and so, technically, they would not receive these labels. It is not like The Hair Club for Men, where the founder is "also a client." However, what Chopra and other New-Age gurus mean by a statement like this is, all of these religious figures were merely misunderstood men and their followers have misinterpreted their common message—that we are all on the same level because everyone really is God. (I can believe a lot of things, but believing I am God has never been a struggle for me.)

3. Jesus lied about being God. Some skeptics believe Jesus was a master of deception. They maintain that in his great desire to be the one to free his Jewish brothers and sisters from the harsh Roman rule, he claimed he was God in an effort to boost his power (the ultimate "fake it till you make it"). Caesar

Augustus had claimed to be the son of God as well, so why not fight fire with fire? According to this view, Jesus manipulatively lied about his identity in order to muster troops for his religious and political revolution. His attempt to fool his disciples and the masses finally caught up with him when the Romans crucified him.

4. Jesus deluded himself into believing he was God. Still another option says that Jesus was delusional. Much like the Charles Mansons and David Koreshes and the many other megalomaniacs of our day, Jesus really believed he was God; he suffered from the original messiah complex. He was actually smoking what he was selling. Many of the greatest innovators and leaders throughout human history have been a little "eccentric," to put it nicely, so why should Jesus be an exception? Though this view is not one of the more popular ones, some do hold to it.

THE BIBLE'S TAKE—AY, THERE'S THE RUB

I know I promised five takes on the idea of Christ's divinity, but before we go to the fifth one, let's take a look at what the Bible and a little common sense have to say on the matter.

1. Jesus *did* claim to be God. Throughout the Gospels, Jesus made many direct and indirect claims to being God in the flesh. In fact, John records one such statement for his own deity that was so strong he was almost killed on the spot.[4] He had told a group of Jewish religious scholars that he lived *before* Abraham. As you probably know, Jews (as well as Christians and Muslims) trace their religious roots back to the Old Testament patriarch Abraham. He is literally hailed as the founding father of Judaism, so you can imagine the scholars' shock and dismay at Christ's declaration. As if this was not enough, he took it a bit further and said this: "Before Abraham lived, I AM." This last statement sent them over the edge.

Now, why in the world would they have wanted to kill

someone for saying that? It seems like nothing more than a grammatical faux pas, but in reality the title Jesus was giving himself was fully loaded. We would have to be Jewish to fully appreciate (or depreciate, rather) what he meant, but knowing some of the history behind this phrase or title will help us to understand the offense a little more. "I AM" is the name God gave himself from the burning bush when he called Moses to bring his people, the Israelites, out of Egypt. Check out this dialogue between them:

> Moses said to God, "Suppose I go to the Isra-elites and say to them, 'The God of your fathers has sent me to you,' and they ask me, 'What is his name?' Then what shall I tell them?"
>
> God said to Moses, "I am who I am. This is what you are to say to the Israelites: 'I AM has sent me to you.'"
>
> God also said to Moses, "Say to the Israelites, 'The LORD, the God of your fathers—the God of Abraham, the God of Isaac and the God of Jacob—has sent me to you.' This is my name for-ever, the name by which I am to be remembered from generation to generation."[5]

So we see that "I AM" is the sacred name of God. To bring it home even more, if I were an orthodox Jew, even today I would not write "I AM." I would not even speak it. All I could do would be to write the initials "YHWH," which stands for "Yahweh," the Hebrew word for "I AM." (In theological circles, these four initials are known as the *tetragrammaton*.) So, if orthodox Jews will not even write or speak this title but actu-ally have to use a symbol and a whole other name for that symbol to refer to it, imagine how horrified these first-century Jews would have felt to hear someone not only speak it—but audaciously own it himself![6]

What amazes me in this passage is that Jesus Christ is not just *admitting* he is divine—he is *forcing* the issue of his divinity on these religious leaders. These are men who would be the least likely and most offended to believe that God could become a man. By the way, this fact alone should shatter any mealy-mouthed, lamb-petting images we have of Jesus.

Perhaps you are still not convinced Jesus claimed to be God and would say that the New Testament could have been embellished by scribes or by political figures, who simply added a mythic layer to Jesus. That's fine—just be aware you will have to go against countless experts in the field of textual criticism and mounds and mounds of ancient documents that chronicle the very events listed in Scripture on which Christ's claim is based. Best of luck to you in that.

> If the disciples had lied about Christ's divinity, they would have had to die *knowing* it was a lie. That makes absolutely no sense.

Or perhaps you like the argument that Christ's disciples beefed up his portfolio after he died and made him into a god in order to save face and give their religious influence a boost. Here's why that doesn't work: Christ's disciples were Jewish. Once again, they would be the last people on the planet to believe that God would become a man. Remember the Jewish leader Saul (later Paul)? His chief goal was to see that all the early Jewish followers of Jesus were put to death. Why? Because Jesus had claimed to be God and, to an unbelieving Jew, that was and is the ultimate blasphemy. In light of such rampant persecution, what did the disciples hope to gain by proclaiming Jesus as Lord and God? Sure imprisonment and death...which is exactly what they got. In fact, all of the original disciples—with the exception of John, who was exiled to the island of Patmos, and Judas, who betrayed Jesus—were killed for this belief.

My point? No one dies for a lie when they know it's a lie. In recent years and all the way to today's newspaper, we see men dying for a lie. But think about it. They don't blow themselves up knowing their religion is a lie; they believe it to be true. If the disciples had lied about Christ's divinity, they would have had to die *knowing* it was a lie. That makes absolutely no sense, especially when you think about the fact that *all* of them died, *and* they died separately, in different parts of the world. For example, it's believed that Thomas (the first empiricist who demanded physical evidence of the resurrection) was martyred on the continent of India, of all places. And even if the disciples did die knowing Christ's divinity was a lie, it's highly unlikely they would all have taken that knowledge to the grave with them, especially not knowing if the others were doing the same.

2. Jesus never wore a crystal. Jesus was a Jewish rabbi. Muslim, Christian, and Jewish scholars (and just plain historians, for that matter) would all agree that Jesus ate, taught, worshiped, and lived as a Jew, speaking to a Jewish community and observing all of its laws. The Jews have always believed there is one God, who created this world and everything in it, and there is a distinct difference between the Creator God and the creature—you and me. Yes, the Bible teaches we are made in the image of God, but it never says we will become God in this age or in the age to come. Furthermore, Jesus taught about resurrection, not reincarnation. To believe this idea of a New-Age Jesus is sort of akin to believing that Elvis and Jimmy Hoffa are fully alive and are playing Ping-Pong on the Moon.

3. Masterful liars are not noble individuals. The idea that Jesus could have deceived his disciples and his multitude of followers into believing he was divine—and that this lie could have been perpetuated for 2000 years—simply will not hold water. Furthermore, nothing about Jesus fits the profile of a liar. Skeptics and believers alike will agree that Jesus was a very noble and good man, as well as a wise teacher. And applying the same logic as we did with his disciples in point number one, if he did lie about his identity and his mission, what did he gain from it anyway? Did he receive more respect? How about riches? No. He was despised, rejected, spat upon, mocked, beaten beyond recognition, and crucified as a criminal. (Liars have a funny way of owning up to the truth when that first nail is being driven in.)

4. Deluded leaders do not produce healthy, moral followers.
The idea that Jesus deluded himself into believing he was God does not pan out either. I'd like to challenge you to name one delusional person in history who has produced healthy, moral followers. Delusional leaders and their followers castrate themselves and die wearing Nikes, waiting for the Hale–Bopp comet to take them on a joyride. Delusional leaders dispense poison-laced Kool-Aid to brainwashed followers in some remote South American jungle. Delusional leaders burn themselves and their devotees to death on farms in Texas. I could go on and on, but let's switch our paths and take a look at Christianity.

Christianity started with a small group of followers in the remote province of Judea. These people were known for their sacrificial love and high moral standards—very attractive qualities in a religion. This last point helps explain the rapid growth that took place. What began as a tiny group in AD 33 expanded to a worldwide movement that had changed the face of the Roman empire by 325. If Jesus Christ had been crazy, history shows that Christianity would have died off with a messy and tragic bang. But it hasn't. Look at what Bono (lead singer for U2...come on, is there really another Bono?) has to say on the issue of Christ's divinity in this excerpt from an interview with French music journalist and friend, Michka Assayas:

Assayas: Christ has his rank among the world's great thinkers. But Son of God, isn't that farfetched?

Bono: No, it's not farfetched to me. Look, the secular
response to the Christ story always goes like this: he
was a great prophet, obviously a very interesting guy,
had a lot to say along the lines of other great prophets,
be they Elijah, Muhammad, Buddha, or Confucius.

But actually Christ doesn't allow you that. He
doesn't let you off that hook. Christ says: No. I'm not
saying I'm a teacher, don't call me teacher. I'm not
saying I'm a prophet. I'm saying: "I'm the Messiah."
I'm saying: "I am God incarnate." And people say:
No, no, please, just be a prophet. A prophet, we can
take. You're a bit eccentric. We've had John the Baptist eating locusts and wild honey, we can handle that.
But don't mention the "M" word! Because, you know,
we're gonna have to crucify you. And he goes: No,
no. I know you're expecting me to come back with an
army, and set you free from these creeps, but actually I
am the Messiah.

At this point, everyone starts staring at their shoes,
and says: Oh, my God, he's gonna keep saying this.
So what you're left with is: either Christ was who He
said He was—the Messiah—or a complete nutcase. I
mean, we're talking nutcase on the level of Charles
Manson. This man was like some of the people we've
been talking about earlier. This man was strapping
himself to a bomb, and had "King of the Jews" on his
head, and, as they were putting him up on the Cross,
was going: "OK, martyrdom, here we go. Bring on the
pain! I can take it." I'm not joking here. The idea that
the entire course of civilization for over half of the
globe could have its fate changed and turned upside-
down by a nutcase, for me, that's farfetched.[7]

THE FINAL TAKE

If you read the New Testament accounts of the life of Jesus,
you come away with this overwhelmingly clear realization—Jesus

was either supernatural or a super nutcase. As we have seen, the super-nutcase option is not viable, so all the evidence points to a fifth and final option: Jesus really was and is God.

I think about the identity of Jesus nearly every day. The belief that God became a man, a human—a baby—is indeed wild and wonderful. I cannot get past this claim, and that is why I am a Christian. Is it difficult to believe? Yes, because it is not simply a matter of looking at the facts (though I realize I may have presented it that way in this chapter). But it also is not a completely blind leap of faith to believe it. It is somewhere in the middle, but no one can explain that to you. If you truly want to get to the bottom of this issue, let me encourage you to do a few things.

First, *read the Gospel of John, and read it with an open mind.* (As if any of us can ever truly be objective…okay, read it with a closed mind if you want, but do read it.) Second, *realize we all believe in things that are paradoxical.* Maybe you'd say, "Believing that Jesus is both God and man does not make sense rationally." Well, take a look at the nature of light for a moment. Scientists have proven that light consist of particles, and they have the empirical data to back it up. Well, scientists have also proven the opposite—that light consists of waves—and they have the empirical data to back this up too. How can both ideas be right? We don't know, but we hold to the reality that they are. Or take quantum mechanics. Here's what one noted physicist says about something known as the Heisenberg uncertainty principle:

> The uncertainty principle protects quantum mechanics. Heisenberg recognized that if it were possible to measure the momentum and position simultaneously with greater accuracy, the quantum mechanics would collapse. So, he proposed that it must be impossible. Then, people sat down and tried to figure out ways of doing it, and nobody could figure out a way to measure the position and

> the momentum of anything—a screen, an electron,
> a billiard ball, anything—with any greater accuracy.
> Quantum mechanics maintains its perilous, but
> accurate, existence.[8]

The Heisenberg uncertainty principle clearly illustrates how often we overlook the little faiths we believe in every day. Bell's theorem and Godel's theorem (which apply to physics and mathematics respectively) illustrate the same idea. It amuses me to no end that we humans will develop complex theorems with complex names—theorems that basically say, "We don't know how these things happen. They seem impossible. But, you know what? They really do happen."

My question is this: Why do we accept paradoxes or "impossibilities" like these but reject the deity of Christ because it seems impossible? Again, remember there are many things we take by faith every single day—like oxygen—because there's no other way to take them. And we aren't aware of them because we're so used to doing it.

Third, *if you do not believe Jesus is God, but you believe he was a good man, then start following his teachings and see what happens.* In other words, truly strive to love your neighbor, give to those who are in need, and forgive those who have hurt you. You will be amazed at what happens when you start trying to live the Jesus way of life. Just try it.

There's no doubt the Jesus way of life has affected millions—probably billions—of people since he came to this earth more than 2000 years ago. Consider these powerful words inspired by a 1926 essay of Dr. James Allan Francis:

> Nearly two thousand years ago in an obscure village, a child was born of a peasant woman. He grew up in another village where He worked as a carpenter until He was thirty. Then for three years He became an itinerant preacher.
>
> This Man never went to college or seminary. He never wrote a book. He never held a public office. He never had a family nor owned a home. He never put His foot inside

a big city nor traveled even 200 miles from His birthplace. And though he never did any of the things that usually accompany greatness, throngs of people followed Him. He had no credentials but Himself.

While He was still young, the tide of public opinion turned against Him. His followers ran away. He was turned over to his enemies and went through the mockery of a trial. He was sentenced to death on a cross between two thieves. While He was dying, His executioners gambled for the only piece of property He had on earth—the simple coat He had worn. His body was laid in a borrowed grave provided by a compassionate friend.

But three days later this Man arose from the dead—living proof that He was, as He had claimed, the Savior whom God had sent, the Incarnate Son of God.

Nineteen centuries have come and gone, and today the risen Lord Jesus Christ is the central figure of the human race. On our calendars His birth divides history in two eras. One day of every week is set aside in remembrance of Him. And our two most important holidays celebrate His birth and resurrection. On church steeples around the world His cross has become the symbol of victory over sin and death.

This one Man's life has furnished the theme for more songs, books, poems and paintings than any other person or event in history. Thousands of colleges, hospitals, orphanages and other institutions have been founded in honor of this One who gave His life for us.

All the armies that ever marched, all the navies that ever sailed, all the governments that ever sat, all the kings that ever reigned have not changed the course of history as much as this One Solitary Life.[9]

That is a compelling commentary, wouldn't you say? It makes us think hard about this issue of Christ's divinity in light of the influence he has had on the world through the ages.

The other day I came upon this passage in Luke, where Jesus asks his followers two questions. The first is this: "Who do the crowds say I am?" In other words, "What do CNN and Fox have to say about my identity?" We can all answer this question. But then Jesus gets personal and asks them this: "Who do you say I am?"[10] That's the question we all have to answer at some time or another. How will you answer?

QUESTIONS TO THINK OVER

1. What is the most staggering claim of Christianity?

2. Explain the significance of Jesus Christ's calling himself "I AM."

3. Explain why it is so unlikely that Christ's disciples could have lied about his identity.

4. Why was Jesus either supernatural or a super nutcase, with no in-between?

5. Try to think of some of the many things we put our faith in day to day without even realizing it.

Part Two

TAKE A DIFFERENT PERSPECTIVE

Chapter 8

For Josh's Eyes Only

* * * * * * * * *

A while ago I was flying from Pensacola, Florida, back to Houston. I was sitting next to a businessman from Connecticut, and we got into a conversation about what we did for a living. I was just returning from one of our youth retreats, where I'd been talking on the subject "Who Am I?" So we got into a little discussion about philosophy, and it kind of meandered into theology. And as my fate would have it, during the course of conversation he found out I was a minister.

This usually shuts down communication right away, but for some reason we were able to continue. One of the things he said to me was this: "I believe your faith is merely a psychological projection." In other words, he believed I have some need for a father figure and that as I've grown older, I've projected this need onto a God I have created in my mind. We went on after that point and dialogued about our different worldviews regarding ethics and how we all got here, and how we're to order and to live our lives. We had a very meaningful conversation. I knew he was thinking hard when he said, "Can you order me another Scotch? This is getting kind of heavy."

Consider your response if you were seated next to the same guy on the plane and he made that challenge to you: "Your faith is merely a psychological projection." How would you answer him? I can tell you that 10 or 15 years ago I was not ready to give a reason for the beliefs I held.

BE PREPARED

Why is it important that we study the philosophies and worldviews of others? Why is it important to be able to give a reasoned and rational defense of what we believe? The Bible challenges us to a greater discipline in understanding our faith and a greater proficiency in communicating that faith to our friends, our family, and the people we work with day to day.

The apostle Peter has something to say about this subject:

> In your hearts set apart Christ as Lord. Always be prepared to give an answer to everyone who asks you to give the reason for the hope that you have. But do this with gentleness and respect.[1]

The Greek word for "answer" is *apologia*. This is where we get the word "apologetics," which is the rational or intellectual defense of a particular belief system. So Peter, one of the original followers of Christ, is saying we need to be prepared to give a defense for not only what we believe, but also why we believe it. And—he says we must be able to give this defense to everyone. His words are still appropriate today.

We live in a time where Christians are bombarded and challenged by *everyone*—relativists, pluralists, nihilists, hedonists, Buddhists, Muslims, Jews, agnostics, atheists, just plain skeptics...and the list goes on. Our society is a smorgasbord of belief systems. In the midst of all this, Peter says, "Listen, as someone who claims to believe in Jesus Christ, you've got to be prepared; as someone who claims to believe in the truth of God's word, you must be ready to give a defense and a reason as to why you believe the way you do."

> **These men and women were eyewitnesses of Christ's resurrection...And what did they do? They gave reasons for the hope they had to anyone and everyone they met.**

If we need more inspiration on the subject, all we need to do is study the first-century disciples as they appear in the book of Acts. These men and women were eyewitnesses of Christ's resurrection. Who were they? Well, they came from all different walks of life. They were fishermen, businessmen, lawyers, tentmakers. And what did they do? They gave reasons for the hope they had to anyone and everyone they met.

Nearly all of the book of Acts gives examples of this. Here are a few:

- Peter says, "Let all Israel be assured of this: God has made this Jesus, whom you crucified, both Lord and Christ."

- Later we read about a recent convert who isn't afraid to defend his newfound faith: "Saul grew more and more powerful and baffled the Jews living in Damascus by *proving* that Jesus is the Christ."

- The apostle Paul went to a public square where people would stand and present different viewpoints all day long, and he spoke in a language they understood, the language of philosophical debate. For instance, he "*reasoned* in the synagogue with the Jews and the God-fearing Greeks, as well as in the marketplace day by day with those who happened to be there."

- Then, "Every Sabbath he reasoned in the synagogue, trying to persuade Jews and Greeks."

- Later, he "entered the synagogue and spoke boldly there for three months, arguing persuasively about the kingdom of God. But some of them became obstinate; they refused to believe and publicly maligned the Way. So Paul left them. He took the disciples with him and had discussions daily in the lecture hall of Tyrannus."[2]

Many more accounts are recorded, but by now we should be seeing that the disciples of the early church left us with an inspiring legacy of faith and boldness in defending the reasons for the hope they had.

GENTLE AND RESPECTFUL ADVICE

Here are five brief pieces of advice for giving a defense with gentleness and respect:

1. Learn the art of listening. Business guru Stephen Covey reformulates some ancient but excellent advice in this phrase: "Seek first to understand, then to be understood." This is especially helpful when talking with someone about your beliefs. Many times Christians try to cram their views down someone's throat without even hearing his or her story. When I was seated by that gentleman on the plane, I would have never gotten that conversation off the ground if I had not chosen to listen before I spoke.

2. Learn the art of asking good questions. I love to ask questions, because I love knowledge and love listening to people's stories. Jesus was great at asking questions. How many times in the Gospels did Christ answer a question directly? Rarely. He usually responded with another question. Ask people (who are interested in talking!), "What is your religious background?" "Why was that important to you?" If someone makes a statement you can't respond to, the best way to answer is with this question: "How do you know that?" Keep asking the "How do you know that?" question about four times in a row and you'll be dealing with ultimate issues—whether you're talking with Stephen Hawking or Steve Martin.

3. Learn the art of passing on a good book. We are all busy. No one has the time to read every book that counters every attack on the Christian faith. (That's one of the reasons the book you're reading is short.) However, you can acquaint yourself with a little knowledge of key books dealing with a variety of issues. For example, if someone is struggling with doubts about the historicity of Jesus, I'm going to point them to books by British scholar N.T. Wright. If someone has questions about evolution or other creation issues, I'm going to point them to books by Hugh Ross or William Dembski. If someone is struggling with philosophic issues, I might point them to books by Gregory Bahnsen or John Frame. If someone doubts the possibility of the resurrection, I'm going to point them to books by Gary Habermas. Christianity has survived for 2000 years not because ladies with pink hair piled to the sky and men with bad toupees peddle "Jesus Junk" on TV, but because Christians have given thoughtful, rational responses to difficult questions skeptics have asked.

4. Learn the art of being normal. Too many times we get really uptight and nervous when we get into a conversation with a skeptic like Mike (especially if Mike is a relative). The best thing you can do is dial down. Take a deep breath. Laugh at yourself. Don't take yourself so seriously. If you really believe in the Christian message, you know you are powerless to change anyone. It's not up to you.

You may be thinking, *What if they ask a question I don't know the answer to?* I've got good news for you—they will. The best way to answer is by saying, "I don't know." Isn't it great to be able to say that? Try it. Besides, God has only revealed a morsel to us in the first place—there is more to come. Sometimes I'll say, "I don't know the answer to that question, but let me recommend a book to you." Or I'll simply say, "I don't know—and no one knows the answer to that question." Everyone lives by faith at some point.

5. Learn the art of being respectful. Some of the greatest people on the planet are Christians, and some of the most obnoxious people on the planet are Christians. When you are talking with someone about ultimate issues—life, death, heaven, hell, God—you are treading on sacred ground. Everyone has a unique story. Be respectful of their story—where they come from, and why they believe what they believe at this point in their journey. If they don't want to talk about these issues, don't talk. If they want to bail out in the middle, let them bail. You may never have the opportunity to tell them all the marvelous truth you know—but that's okay. As Saint Francis of Assisi explained to his disciples, "Preach always. If necessary, use words."

Chapter 9

For Mike's Eyes Only

● ● ● ● ● ● ● ● ●

I don't know if a friend or relative gave you this book or you picked it up at a local bookstore or online, but thanks for taking the time to read it. Since we're into reality-TV shows so much these days, I thought you might appreciate a real-life Mike-and-Josh scenario. The following is a true story about a friend of mine—a former agnostic—and his journey to Christianity.

A NOT-SO-LIGHT LUNCH

I first met Rick Smalley in Houston on April 13, 2004. I had been invited by Jim Tour (remember the scientist from chapter 4?) to have lunch with him and Rick at Rice University's Faculty Club. To give a little background: Rick had been going to the church where I'm a pastor for almost three months because his girlfriend, Debbie—who was a Christian and whom Rick later married—had suggested it. The two of them had been sampling different churches together, and Debbie thought they should try out the church that Preston, Rick's eight-year-old son, liked.

So Jim, Rick, and I sat down to lunch, and after some not-so-small talk, Rick said, "You know, Ben, when I first started coming to your service, I was repulsed." I knew right away I was going to like this guy—a straight-shooter. Then he said, "Ben, tell me...you said Jesus came back to life. What did you mean by 'came back to life'? Brainwave, heartbeat? You talked about Jesus having a resurrected body—tell me a little bit about that resurrected body. What did it consist of? What did it feel like?" We talked about continuity and discontinuity, and I tried to unpack all of it in the best way I knew how.

Then Rick made a very simple yet profound statement—one that really encapsulated his "little adventure,"[1] as he liked to call it: "What I am really trying to figure out right now is, what makes Christianity so powerful?" I thought, *Wow, an academic with the boldness to explore what's become taboo in so many university settings.* And so began a friendship and a dialogue that changed both of our lives in many ways.

AN INTELLECTUAL'S QUEST

This 1996 Nobel laureate was searching for answers—ones that made scientific sense. I knew Rick was in good company with Jim Tour. Rick knew Jim well and respected him; he'd actually recruited Jim around six years before from the University of South Carolina. Over most of that time, Rick had shown no curiosity about Christianity, but lately, he'd been taking more notice of Jim's personal life. Jim had a wonderfully functional and loving family—something Rick had always wanted but that seemed to elude him. He suspected Christianity might have something to do with this...but wasn't too comfortable with the idea.

In August 2004, he heard Jim give a talk at my church on the amazing power of Scripture, in which Jim mentioned getting up at 5:30 every morning to read the Bible and pray. Rick was skeptical about the purpose and benefit of such a practice. Though part of his weekends with Debbie included discussions on the Bible and the sermons they heard, he still wasn't buying that the Bible was the true Word of God and was beginning to feel stuck in disbelief.

That's when Hugh Ross entered the mix.* Jim invited Hugh to speak at Rice University in September 2004. Rick, along with Debbie, spoke with Hugh for a couple of hours before attending his three-hour lecture and question-and-answer session. During their meeting before the lecture, they were free to ask Hugh any question, no matter how far out it seemed. Debbie, a scientist and biology teacher herself, asked Hugh some questions she knew Rick had been struggling with regarding science and its compatibility with Christianity. Rick was really impressed with the answers Hugh gave.

Slightly later, while they were listening to Hugh's lecture, Rick leaned over to Jim's wife and asked, "Is there anything that this guy doesn't know?" This evening with Hugh Ross made a great impact on Rick. He was fascinated. (In fact, he was so keyed up, he ran three miles nonstop at 11 PM. Pretty intense for a 61-year old, but he was in tip-top shape—his cancer was in remission.)

Rick went on to develop his very own lecture from the notes he furiously took during Hugh's. Here are some excerpts from the "cheat sheet" Rick made for a speech he gave at Tuskegee University on October 3, 2004:

> I will tell them that science has now shown that Genesis is amazingly correct in its story of creation (how could Moses have known?)...I will tell them that the universe is now known to be exquisitely fine tuned to enable life, and that

---

* Hugh Ross, PhD—an astrophysicist formerly of CalTech Jet Propulsion Laboratory—has written extensively on the Bible being the only accurate explanation for the origin of the universe, the origin of life, and the reasons for their existence that match with the fossil record and astrophysical evidence. He founded the organization Reasons to Believe, which you can read about at www.reasons.org.

> our universe is either a random choice among at least 10^{60} other universes, none of the rest of which could possibly have supported life, or it was built this way by some master creator. It was built for life...
>
> While we know that all life is intimately related and has evolved from a single common ancestor cell, proliferating one species after another over the past 3.85 billion years, it is not at all clear that this evolution could have happened as it did without divine intervention...Let's do what we have been put here on Earth to do in this very, very special time.[2]

Rick got a standing ovation for this lecture, but perhaps the most amazing thing about it is how his formerly antagonistic views about belief in the God of the Bible had changed.

THE ASTROPHYSICIST
AND THE NOBEL LAUREATE

Rick had been inspired and began devouring Hugh's writings. He read at least five of his books. In fact, after reading *Who Is Adam?*—then Hugh's latest book—he declared, "If the scientific community read that book, 50 percent of them would become Christians." But I'm getting ahead of the story now.

So Hugh and Rick became friends and e-mail buddies. Rick respected Hugh's ability to answer his questions with theological *and* scientific depth. Hugh gives us insight into some of their discussions here:

> I knew ahead of time that Rick was a stickler for scientific credibility and integrity. I expected him to besiege me with questions about biological evolution, or about Bible passages that he presumed were in conflict with science. What I learned was, that Rick loved to research frontiers of knowledge that few before him had ever probed. The thrill of Rick's life was to explore, and to invent.

You know, others have asked me about God's purpose in creating the universe, and humanity. Rick already had perceived that if God does exist, he must have more than one purpose in creating. So, we talked about God's seven different purposes in creating the universe. In light of these seven purposes, Rick wanted to know exactly what we humans are supposed to do. He wanted to know why this God that created the universe would grant us free will. He had already concluded that there is no resolution of human free will and Divine pre-determination within the dimensions of length, width, height and time. He asked me if the extra dimensions implied by string theory and general relativity provided possible resolutions. (By the way, they really do.)

We discussed God's plan for ridding His creation of evil; and how we humans benefit from the evil that we now currently experience. He asked about the purpose of mass extinction events in the fossil record, the purpose of death, the reason for short life spans, and what life will be like in the New Creation.

Now, most scientists I know allow peer pressure, and their specialized research endeavors, to divert them from probing the most important issues of the cosmos, and of life. I found this especially to be the case with Nobel laureates; but Rick was different. He had the humility, and the courage, to pursue the "big truth" questions—regardless of personal cost to his reputation.[3]

Think about it: If you presume you have it all figured out, how can you approach science...or anything else with the intent to analyze and learn about it?

Rick's questioning continued, and so did his journey towards Christianity. You see, a cutting-edge scientist has the ability to see things that are unseen—if the humility is there. He had the humility. Really, it was that humility that enabled him from the beginning to go through all those uncharted scientific territories he's famous for discovering. (Think about it: If you presume you have it all figured out, how can you approach science, art, literature, philosophy, music, or anything else with the intent to analyze and learn about it? Any intellectual endeavor we take on must begin with humility.) Earlier in his research, when he was talking about what would later be called "buckyballs,"* some skeptics were saying, "They don't really exist. That is not really going to happen." Of course, that didn't deter the courageous Rick Smalley. He and his colleagues just kept digging and working and sweating, and it all paid off.

He took that same humble, analytical, and tenacious (also known as stubborn) mind he'd used to explore every scientific aspect of the universe he could—and applied it to a "re-investigation of Christianity" (his words) and what made it so powerful.

A PRIZE GREATER THAN THE NOBEL?

In June of 2005, Rick began getting up at five-thirty every morning to read the Bible, as he'd heard Jim Tour speak of doing almost a year earlier. He started in the first chapter of Genesis and went all the way through the last chapter of Revelation, from beginning to end. When he finished his first read-through, he started over again (talk about *tenacious!*). And he said the

---

* Rick Smalley is probably best known for his discovery of the spherical fullerene C_{60}, a soccer-ball-shaped molecule commonly known as a *buckyball*. Perhaps the most exciting characteristic of the buckyball is that it is hollow on the inside, and Smalley insisted that all elements in the periodic table would fit inside. This could create any number of practical uses, the most notable being in the field of medicine. Drugs could be administered molecularly—or more importantly, individual radioactive molecules could be contained within the buckyball. Scientists are now developing these "loaded" buckyballs, which will attack cancer and other diseases more accurately and precisely.

more he read it, the more convinced he was of the intellectual veracity revealed in Scripture. Here's another comment from Hugh Ross, this one regarding Rick's take on the Bible:

> I know from my conversations and e-mails with Rick over the past year, this last year of his life was his most thrilling as a scientist. In his words, he learned that "he need not throw his mind away when reading the Bible." The Bible made him an even better scientist, and a more inspiring science educator.[4]

It was some time during the "past year" Hugh speaks of that Rick made the transition from simply believing in God as a creator—or a force—to really trusting him: trusting Christ to rule his life. Like C.S. Lewis and other intellectuals who walked the same path as Rick, I think his "head" believed before his "heart"—only God truly knows. But it's not the order that counts.

GRADUATION

It was my honor to know Rick for what was too brief a time. His death seemed early considering the further good to humanity his research in nanotechnology would have yielded had he been given a little more time. On October 28, 2005, after a seven-year battle with leukemia, Rick continued his quest for truth on the other side of this life. We are all the better for his life and contribution to science. I am the better for his friendship and having experienced his courage to never stop seeking truth. This book is dedicated to his memory.

Yes, scientists from all backgrounds are believers—and, yes, scientists from all backgrounds are unbelievers. The lives of other Nobel laureates might present an entirely different story.

This was Rick's story: his journey to the Christian faith...or its journey to him. Why do I share such a story with you? I share it to assure you that you never have to park your brain to be a Christian. I also share it to encourage you in your own quest for the truth.

WHAT YOU CAN LEARN FROM RICK'S JOURNEY

1. He had the courage and the humility to seek answers to his questions. Many people just dismiss Christianity before investigating because they're afraid of how believing it might change their lives. Rick read the Bible through, asked questions, read books, and asked more questions. It *did* change his life. From what you just read, do you think he regretted it?

2. He observed the lives of others and sought to connect the dots between what they *did* and what they *believed.* In so doing, he was able to see what true Christianity is because it was lived out by his wife and by other close friends. This made a huge impact on him. It's one thing to theorize abstractly—it's quite another to see real love in action.

3. Like so many others, he saw that the Christian worldview was both "rational and romantic," as C.S. Lewis put it. In other words, the intellectual depth of the Bible and the existential peace that Rick—and Lewis—experienced were compatible.

Back to Barbecue

* * * * * * * * * *

Mike: So why are you dressed up?

Josh: I went to church this morning.

Mike: What kind of church?

Josh: It's nondenominational—just a Christian church.

Mike: Interesting. I had no idea you were a Bible-thumper. [He chuckles.]

Josh: Well, I definitely believe in the Bible, but I'm not into pushing my beliefs on others.

Mike: Good for you, man! I get so tired of those folks who feel the need to convert everybody. I think it just shows weakness on their part.

Josh: How so?

Mike: It just seems like they're afraid to stand alone—almost like they need affirmation for what they believe. We all have our own individual beliefs. What's true and right for one person isn't necessarily true for the next.

Josh: Hmm. So what do you believe?

Mike: I personally believe if you're a good person, you're going to be all right, whatever your idea of "all right" is. We're all here just trying to do our best, you know? To me, it shouldn't matter what path you take. None of us really *knows* what the truth is anyway. And if there really is a God, I can't imagine him condemning people for not believing one particular way. That just wouldn't be fair. It makes me so mad when these self-righteous Christians claim they're the only ones going to "heaven." You say you're a Christian—do *you* really believe Jesus Christ is the only way to God?

Josh: Yes, I do.

Mike: So you would condemn all the Jews, Muslims, Hindus, and the rest of the moral population just because they don't see Jesus as the Son of God?

Josh: I don't really think it's my place to condemn anyone, but I do know that Jesus is "the way, the truth, and the life." The Bible says it's only through him that any of us can get to God the Father.

Mike: Look, Josh, any educated person knows the Bible isn't really true. Evolution proved that a long time ago. I've read my fair share of the Bible and, sure, we can glean a modicum of wisdom from its tales and proverbs—just like any other ancient writing—but do you honestly think all that stuff really happened? The Bible is basically a bunch of myths. My grandmother was a Christian, and she used to tell us stories from the Bible. Let me ask you: How is a talking donkey plausible? That one was my favorite.

Josh: It was a miracle.

Mike: Miracles like that don't happen these days, and if they don't happen now, why would they have happened then?

Josh: People are miraculously healed of all sorts of diseases all the time. How do you account for that?

Mike: They just got lucky, in my opinion. What about all the people who *don't* get healed—people who've got entire churches praying for them? Why wouldn't God heal them? That seems so arbitrary.

Josh: Well, Mike, he's God—his ways are too lofty for us to understand.

Mike: And you buy that? That is such a cop-out, Josh. Figure something out for yourself. Give me a reason, without regurgitating what you learned in Sunday school. Remember, I don't believe in the Bible. You can't keep using it for your arguments. Give me a rational explanation, please.

Josh: Well, I take the Bible as the foundation for all truth. Asking me to stop using it in my arguments is like asking someone to speak without vocal cords.

Mike: Well, I guess we're done with our little discussion then. [He gives a victorious laugh.]

Josh: If you don't want to believe, it's your choice. I just want you to recognize what you're really claiming.

Mike: What are you talking about?

Josh: Recognize that in choosing to reject the Bible's good news, you are assuming the position of God in your own life.

Mike: Okay, so what's wrong with that? It's my life, Josh.

Josh: Well, if you are your own authority, then what will be your foundation for right and wrong, for morality and ethics?

Mike: I know what's right and wrong. I'm a good person. I

treat others as I like to be treated. I don't steal, kill, or covet my neighbor's wife.

Josh: Okay, it's obvious you're mocking me now by quoting from the Ten Commandments, but think about it—are you not borrowing from my Christian worldview to furnish ethics for your own?

Mike: What?

Josh: Let me put it this way: Can you come up with any "moral" behavior that is not found directly in Scripture?

Mike: Hmm...I guess not. But so what? The Bible was written by men who just felt the same way I do.

Josh: But where does that morality come from, Mike?

Mike: From inside of us. I believe that all people desire in their heart of hearts to do good to their fellow man—or at least to treat others as they'd like to be treated.

Josh: Wow, you must not watch the news. How do you account for evil in the world if all men are basically good?

Mike: I don't know...society is corrupt.

Josh: Come on, Mike, you're not going to pull the whole "noble savage" thing on me now. Are you honestly saying civilization is the culprit? If you take civilization away, all the good it's done will have to go too... advances in modern technology, in medicine, in education.

Mike: Well, I guess I don't know where evil comes from. Maybe some people are just innately bad.

Josh: You do realize you're contradicting what you said thirty seconds ago...that all people are basically good?

Mike: I guess I just don't have it all figured out just yet. Maybe being *God* isn't as easy as I thought. [His tone is sarcastic.]

Josh: That's why God is *God*—and we're not.

Mike: Okay, okay, I'll indulge you a minute. Let's say God, or an ultimate authority, does exist. I still don't understand why this God would allow evil at all. He can't be a good God then.

Josh: Well, would you say we all have free will—that is, the ability to choose what we want to do, where we want to go, or how we want to believe in life?

Mike: Yes—so?

Josh: And wouldn't you say that in that ability lies the power to choose something that would affect another person?

Mike: Yes, it's quite obvious our choices affect one another.

Josh: Well, how could God allow you to choose something that would be good for others but then disallow you to choose something bad for others? That's not really the freedom to choose, is it?

Mike: I guess not.

Josh: And do you see how truly good and loving it is of God to protect our free will so much that he even allows us not to believe in him or in his Son?

Mike: Okay, you may have been getting me to budge a little on the existence of God. I'm not a close-minded person, but this "Son of God" business is a little far-fetched, wouldn't you say? Jesus was a good man, but it stops there.

Josh: A good man who boldly claimed to be God in the flesh. How do you get around that?

Mike: Well, *if* he did really claim that, it seems to me he must have been deluded.

Josh: I like your line of reasoning. It really does come down to that. Either Jesus was crazy, or he is who he said he was. And thanks to your God-given free will, it's your

choice on whether or not to believe it. But let me ask
you a question. What's more difficult to believe, that
one single crazy person changed the course of human
history forever and shaped civilization as we know it
and that millions of people are still interpreting and
trying to follow his words—or that Jesus really was and
is the Son of God?

Mike: Good question.

Well, I'd have to say Josh did a lot better this time around.
Mike may not have been altogether convinced, but Josh
definitely gave him something to chew on besides his brisket
sandwich, and that's all that could be asked of him. Hopefully,
Mike will come away from their discussion thinking a little bit
more about what he really believes.

If you consider yourself a skeptic, I hope you'll do the same
thing after having read this book. Examine your own reasons
for rejecting what the Bible says and see what's at the root. In
my experience, I've found that more than any of the other
Mike-like reasons, there are three primary reasons people reject
the good news about Jesus.

"INTELLECTUAL" REASONS

If you are educated today in our public-school system, if
you go to college and get a degree, or if you're simply a con-
sumer of mass media, then you undoubtedly have been fed the
idea that becoming a Christian is equivalent to committing
intellectual suicide. It goes something like this: "No thinking
person, no intelligent person, would ever believe in the Bible
or in miracles or in anything silly like that." I see and hear this
way of thinking on the radio, on TV, and in various kinds of
literature on a daily basis. The truth of the matter is, some of

the greatest minds in history and in our world today were and are "born-again" Christians.

Those who hold so firmly to the belief that Christians are neither intelligent nor cultured have apparently never heard of J.R.R. Tolkien (well, now they have, thanks to Peter Jackson), C.S. Lewis, Hugh Ross, J. Budziszewski, Cornelius Plantinga, or the many other Christian intellects, philosophers, astrophysicists, biologists, psychologists, psychiatrists, lawyers, authors, doctors, and artists.

No, what they see are the debates on CNN, *Crossfire,* or *Donahue,* with "Mr. or Ms. Two-PhDs-from-Harvard" against "Billy Bob, the Backwoods Baptist." We've all seen it; it concludes something like this: "Well, Phil—God said it, I believe it, that settles it!" What results is a cartoon-character representation of what it means to be a Christian (and this person speaks for all Christians, of course) being pitted against a very calm and rational intellectual. These "debates" only affirm the already prevalent idea that people of faith and people of facts are polar opposites. (You can also watch a lot of the junk that passes for "Christian TV." The gold-leafed gospel that some—not all—of these people sell is enough to make *me* a skeptic. Unfortunately, these people only validate many of the "intellectual" reasons skeptics cite for rejecting the good news.)

REASONS OF A PSYCHOLOGICAL NATURE

I had a conversation with a professing atheist years ago, and I remember asking him, "Why don't you believe in God?" He went straight down the classic arguments for not believing in God: "Well, first of all, there is so much evil and suffering in the world, how can anyone believe in God? If there is a God, he is not a good God. Second of all, look at science and evolution. Haven't they proven that the God of Scripture, the Christian God, is not true? We have no need for deity anymore. And look at the great diversity of religions and pluralistic belief systems we have today. I mean, are you really saying all these people are wrong and you're right? What about the people who have never heard this message? What's going to happen to them?"

After talking with him for a while about all these issues, I asked him, "Mike [not his real name], what was it like growing up in your house?" He said, "Well, I never really knew my dad. When I was two years old, he left us." He went on to describe how his views of life and of love had been severely damaged by this event. "Mike," I told him in conclusion, "I believe I can lead you to some answers to the questions and doubts you have about God and the Christian faith. By no means do I have all the answers, but I have books—and I know some people who have a lot more knowledge than I have, and I think they'll be able to help you out. But I believe that in the long run you're going to see that your real reason for rejecting God and Christ is not any of the initial reasons you brought up. You're going to see that when your dad left you as a kid, somehow, in your heart and your mind, God left you too."

Consider the intriguing book *Faith of the Fatherless.* Its subtitle is *The Psychology of Atheism,* and in this book New York University professor Dr. Paul C. Vitz goes back and looks at the childhoods of some of the most famous modern-day atheists, including philosophers, writers, and political leaders. The results are astounding. Let's look at a few of them:

- *Friedrich Nietzsche* was the son of a Lutheran pastor. When Friedrich was only four years old, his father died. Later he would go on to write some incredible works of philosophy. He became an atheist, making the famous pronouncement, "God is dead." One biographer said that Nietzsche's whole body of work could be classified as a quest for a father.

- *Bertrand Russell,* the brilliant Nobel Prize–winning mathematician and philosopher from England, lost both of his parents when he was four. In his later years he wrote a book entitled *Why I Am Not a Christian,* which was really a series of essays expressing his vehement opposition to theism and especially to Christianity.

- *Jean-Paul Sartre,* the existentialist, lost his father when he was 15 months old. In his writings he said fathers could be burdensome, and eventually the worst ones would end up stifling and crushing their children. He saw fatherless people like himself as having a sense of "lightness" and as the only people who could make an authentic choice to live their lives as they saw fit.

- Another existentialist, *Albert Camus,* also lost his father when he was just one year old. The whole concept of the father became the preoccupation of his work.

- *Sigmund Freud's* father, Jacob, was a great disappointment to his son because Sigmund's mother and her family had to provide the financial sustenance for the family. Freud also despised his father's passive stance towards anti-Semitism, as well as his tendency towards sexual perversion. As a result, in his later years, Freud put hatred of the father at the center of his proposed Oedipus complex; he also blamed his loss of religion on the breakdown of his father's authority in his life.

You can look at political leaders like Adolf Hitler, Mao Zedong, and Josef Stalin and find an abusive and destructive father. Paul Vitz concludes that some of the most influential atheists of our day were products of weak, dead, or abusive fathers.[1]

IF I CLOSE MY EYES, IT WILL DISAPPEAR

The last and primary reason I believe people reject what the Bible says is simply because they don't want it to be true. The fact is, God has revealed himself to the world and to all humans. One way he has done this is through his creation. Another, as we saw in chapter 1, is through the conscience—or sense of morality—he has woven into the fabric of every person.

The lifestyle you've chosen and the perspective you're seeking to live by right now—is it working for you?

Many people, though, take this innate knowledge of God, our Creator, and try to suppress it because they simply don't want him to exist. Like Mike, they don't want to have to answer to anyone but themselves. Take a look at what Aldous Huxley, author of the famous book *Brave New World*, says elsewhere:

> I had motives for not wanting the world to have a meaning; consequently I assumed that it had none, and was able without any difficulty to find satisfying reasons for this assumption.... For myself, as, no doubt, for most of my contemporaries, the philosophy of meaninglessness was essentially an instrument of liberation. The liberation we desired was simultaneously liberation from a certain political and economic system and liberation from a certain system of morality. We objected to the morality because it interfered with our sexual freedom.[2]

And check out this quote from Thomas Nagel, a professor of philosophy at New York University:

> I want atheism to be true and am made uneasy by the fact that some of the most intelligent and well-informed people I know are religious believers. It isn't just that I don't believe in God and, naturally, hope that I'm right in my belief.

It's that I hope that there is no God! I don't want there to be a God; I don't want the universe to be like that.[3]

Why do they reject faith in God? These very intelligent, rational thinkers boldly admit they simply do not *want* to believe. I appreciate their honesty.

It all comes to this: Acknowledging there is a Higher Power than ourselves forces us to relinquish the autonomy we hold so dear. And this isn't easy for anybody, whether you're a Mike, a Josh—or a Jennifer who's somewhere in the middle. But here's the real question: The lifestyle you've chosen and the perspective you're seeking to live by right now—is it working for you?

- Do you measure up to the standards you set for yourself?

- Do you feel shame and guilt when you don't?

- Do you find yourself longing for acceptance...but you're not sure from where?

- Do you have healthy intimate relationships, or do you feel disconnected?

- Do you experience a sense of emptiness no matter how much fun you have or how much money or things you attain?

- Do you truly have meaning and a sense of purpose in your life?

Essentially, Christianity is not about engaging in philosophical debate, though there are many places and times when this is necessary and appropriate. And it is important to know there are reasonable responses to most any argument against Christianity you can think of. (By no means am I implying they're all in this book—this is only the tip of a gigantic iceberg. If you have other questions, see the items listed under "More Resources," and look for other resources as well—we should never give up in our quest for truth.)

At some point, however, you've got to realize that—at its heart—Christianity calls for a personal response from you. It's both an invitation and a joyous announcement.

God is saying to you and to me: "Come to my son, and I will set you free. Stop trying to go it alone. It's not every man for himself, every woman for herself. I've given myself for everyone."

More Resources

* * * * * * * * * *

Always Ready: Directions for Defending the Faith by G.L. Bahnsen

Between Heaven and Hell by Peter Kreeft

Can Man Live Without God by Ravi Zacharias

Every Thought Captive: A Study Manual for the Defense of Christian Truth by Richard L. Pratt

God the Evidence: The Reconciliation of Faith and Reason in a Postsecular World by Patrick Glynn

Miracles by C.S. Lewis

Relativism: Feet Firmly Planted in Mid-Air by Francis J. Beckwith, Gregory Koukl

The Case for Faith: A Journalist Investigates the Toughest Objections to Christianity by Lee Strobel

The Design Revolution: Answering the Toughest Questions About Intelligent Design by William A. Dembski

The Question of God: C.S. Lewis and Sigmund Freud Debate God, Love, Sex, and the Meaning of Life by Dr. Armand Nicholi Jr.

The Universe Next Door by James Sire

The Truth Behind the Da Vinci Code: A Challenging Response to the Bestselling Novel by Richard Abanes

True for You, but Not for Me: Deflating the Slogans That Leave Christians Speechless by Paul Copan

Who Was Adam?: A Creation Model Approach to the Origin of Man by Fazale Rana, Hugh Ross

Without a Doubt: Answering the 20 Toughest Faith Questions by Ronald Nash (Foreword), Kenneth Richard Samples

Notes

* * * * * * * * *

Mike's Barbecue

1. John 14:6.

Chapter 1—Because It's True for You, But Not for Me

1. The Barna Research Group, Ltd., "Americans Are Most Likely to Base Truth on Feelings," www.barna.org, February 12, 2002.

2. Adapted from a story by Paul Copan as found online.

3. Paul Copan, *True for You, But Not for Me* (Minneapolis, MN: Bethany House Publishers, 1998), p. 22. Copan is paraphrasing a selection from Friedrich Nietzsche's "The Gay Science," *The Portable Nietzsche*, Walter Kaufman, ed. and trans. (New York: Viking, 1954), p. 95.

4. Romans 2:14-15.

5. Romans 1:20-21.

6. John 14:6.

7. For more on this idea, see Louis Berkhof's take on common grace at www.mbrem.com.

Chapter 2—Because All Paths Lead to God

1. LaTonya Taylor, "The Church of O," *Christianity Today*, April 1, 2002, p. 38.

2. T. Keller and C. Garland, *The Current Intellectual State of Affairs in America:* "Philosophical & Religious Pluralism," June 20, 2003.

3. See Romans 3:21-24.

Chapter 3—Because All Christians Are Hypocrites

1. Matthew 23:27-28.

2. Facts 1 through 3 are loosely based on Frank Harber, *Reasons for Believing* (Green Forest, AR: New Leaf Press, 1998), pp. 143-147.

Chapter 4—Because Evolution Is True

1. Patrick Glynn, *GOD: The Evidence* (Rocklin, CA: Prima Publishing, 1997), pp. 2-3.

2. Definition of Intelligent Design, "Intelligent Design and the Theory of Evolution," www.wordiq.com, 2004.

3. A quote from Stephen J. Gould, courtesy of David Friend and the editors of *Life Magazine*, "The Meaning of Life" (1991) p. 33, as quoted in Ravi Zacharias, *Can Man Live Without God?* (Nashville, TN: W Publishing Group, 1994), p. 31.

4. Taken from James Tour's résumé at www.jmtour.com, last updated March 9, 2006.

5. James Tour, personal interview at Second Baptist Church, Houston, TX, January 27, 2003.

6. Taken from William Dembski's résumé at www.iscid.org, last updated 2003.

7. William Dembski, personal interviews at Baylor University, Waco, TX, November 19 and 20 and December 13, 2002.

8. A statement from Dr. Hugh Ross about the Kansas School Board decision on the Big Bang from http://www.astro.ucla.edu/~wright/cosmo-religion.html (1999-2005 Edward L. Wright, last modified 10 October, 2005).

9. James Tour.

Chapter 5—Because the Bible Is Full of Myths

1. Much of this chapter was influenced by Peter Kreeft, *Between Heaven and Hell* (Madison, WI: InterVarsity Press, 1982), pp. 75-80.

2. British author Colin Duriez, who wrote the article "Tollers and Jack" in issue #78 of *Christian History,* explains why this is so in his book *Tolkien and C.S. Lewis: The Gift of Friendship* (Hidden Spring). Duriez tells the story of how these two brilliant authors met, discovered their common love for mythical tales, and pledged to bring such stories into the mainstream of public reading taste. *Christian History* managing editor Chris Armstrong reached Duriez at his home in Leicester, England, for this interview.

3. *The Simpsons,* "Much Apu About Nothing" (from season 7), as found at Science Fair Projects Encyclopedia Page, "Correlation implies causation (logical fallacy)," www.all-science-fair-projects.com, last updated September 20, 2004.

4. Dr. Gregory Bahnsen uses this line of argumentation in his epic 1985 debate with Dr. Gordon Stein, the former editor of *Skeptic Magazine.*

5. Helmut Koester, *History and Literature of Early Christianity,* 2 vols. (Philadelphia: Fortress, 1982), vol. 2, pp. 16–17.

6. John A.T. Robinson, *Can We Trust the New Testament?* (Grand Rapids, MI: Eerdmans, 1977), p. 36. Atheist Antony Flew agrees in Gary R. Habermas and Antony G. N. Flew, *Did Jesus Rise from the Dead? The Resurrection Debate,* ed. Terry L. Miethe (San Francisco: Harper & Row, 1987), p. 66.

7. The *Times* (London, England), www.soon.org.uk/page19.htm, referenced March 22, 2006.

8. From pages 17, 18. "The Gospel Standard," Vol. 44, no. 1, September 1994. (Published by the "Peoples Gospel Hour," Box 1660, Halifax, N.S. B3J 3A1.)

9. Richard N. Ostling, "Prophet or Pretender: Bicentennial of Mormon church founders' birth renews debate" (Associated Press).

10. Michael Guillen, *Can a Smart Person Believe in God?* (Nashville, TN: Nelson Books, 2004), p. 2.

11. Adapted from Richard Pratt, "A Deconstruction of Mary Had a Little Lamb," a talk given at Second Baptist Church, Houston, TX, March 7, 2003.

Chapter 6—Because of Evil and Suffering

1. David Hume, *Dialogues Concerning Natural Religion: Part X* (1779), www.philosophy ofreligion.info/hume.html, March 22, 2006.

2. Greg L. Bahnsen, *Always Ready: Directions for Defending the Faith* (Nacogdoches, TX: Covenant Media Press, 1996), p. 171.

3. Ravi Zacharias, *Can Man Live Without God?* (Nashville, TN: W Publishing Group), pp. 182-183.

4. Hebrews 11:17-19.

5. Deuteronomy 29:29.

6. See Job 38–39.

7. Gregory Koukl, "Littleton, CO: Where Was God?" www.str.org/site/News2?page=Ne wsArticle+ID=5437, referenced March 25, 2006.

8. Ann Henderson Hart, "Finding Hope Beyond the Ruins: An Interview with Lisa Beamer," *Modern Reformation* magazine, September/October 2002, pp. 24-31.

Chapter 7—Because Jesus Was Just a Good Man

1. Dan Brown, *The Da Vinci Code* (New York, NY: Doubleday, a division of Random House, Inc., 2003), p. 233.

2. Brown, p. 234.

3. Mark 8:29.

4. See John 8:58.

5. Exodus 3:13-15.

6. Here are some more instances of Christ's boldly stating his divinity: In John 10:30, Jesus says, "I and the Father are one." In John 14:9, he tells Philip, "Anyone who has seen me has seen the Father." Another is found in John 11:25-26, where he says: "I am the resurrection and the life...whoever lives and believes in me will never die." Did you catch that? He is claiming to give eternal life. Then in John 14:6, a famous passage, he points to himself and says, "I am the way and the truth and the life. No one comes to the Father except through me." He does not say, "I am *a* way," but "*the* way." And these are just from the book of John. If you want other passages that relate to the divinity of Christ, check out Matthew 2:11; Mark 12:6; Luke 10:22; John 1:1; Romans 9:5; Colossians 2:9; and Revelation 22:13.

7. From "Bono: Grace over Karma," www.christianitytoday.com, posted 08/08/05. Book excerpt from *Bono: In Conversation with Michka Assayas,* by Michka Assayas.

8. Richard P. Feynman, *Six Easy Pieces: Essentials of Physics Explained by Its Most Brilliant Teacher* (Reading, MA: Addison-Wesley, 1994), p. 138.

9. Adapted by www.word4life.com from the original essay by Dr. James Allan Francis in *The Real Jesus and Other Sermons* (Philadelphia: The Judson Press, 1926), pp. 123-124.

10. See Luke 9:18-20.

Chapter 8—For Josh's Eyes Only

1. 1 Peter 3:15.

2. Acts 2:76; 9:22; 17:17; 18:4; 19:8.

Chapter 9—For Mike's Eyes Only

1. See Mark Lisheron, "Rewiring the World: All too aware of his own mortality, a Nobel winner is racing to help solve humankind's problems," www.statesman.com, *American-Statesman*, April 11, 2004.

2. Richard E. Smalley, Ph.D., Annual Scholarship Convocation, Tuskegee University, October 3, 2004.

3. Hugh Ross, "Celebrating the Life of Richard Smalley, Ph.D.," transcript of eulogy given at Second Baptist Church, Houston, Texas, November 2, 2005.

4. Ross.

Back to Barbecue

1. Paul C. Vitz, *Faith of the Fatherless: The Psychology of Atheism* (Dallas, TX: Spence Publishing Company, 1999), pp. 20, 26-31, 47-48, 104-107.

2. Aldous Huxley, *Ends and Means: An Inquiry into the Nature of Ideas and into the Methods Employed for Their Realization* (London/New York: Chatto & Windus/Harper & Brothers, 1937), pp. 270-273.

3. Thomas Nagel, as quoted by J. Budziszewski, "The Second Tablet Project," *First Things*, June/July 2002, p. 28.

OTHER BOOKS BY BEN YOUNG

Cowritten with Dr. Sam Adams

Out of Control: Finding Peace for the Physically Exhausted and Spiritually Strung Out

The Ten Commandments of Dating: Time-Tested Laws for Building Successful Relationships

The Ten Commandments of Dating (Student Edition): Time-Tested Laws for Building Successful Relationships

The One: A Realistic Guide to Choosing Your Soul Mate

Devotions for Dating Couples: Building a Foundation for Spiritual Intimacy

Cowritten with Glenn Lucke

Common Grounds: Conversations About the Things That Matter Most

TO CONTACT BEN YOUNG
FOR A SPEAKING ENGAGEMENT

Ben Young
Second Baptist Church
6400 Woodway
Houston, TX 77057

www.benyoung.org
trichmond@second.org
713.465.3408

An eye-opening resource about spiritual truth in the Superman saga and our culture's entertainment

The Gospel According to the World's Greatest Superhero

STEPHEN SKELTON

From above, a heavenly father sends his only son to save the Earth...

Sound familiar? It should—whether you're a fan of Superman or a reader of the Bible. Did you know...

- that Superman film and television writers have confirmed they modeled the superhero on Christ?

- that Superman's earthly parents were originally named "Mary" and "Joseph"?

- that Superman movies, TV shows, and comics contain deliberate parallels to Jesus' death, burial, and resurrection—and even his second coming?

Fearless Faith
Living Beyond the Walls of Safe Christianity

JOHN FISCHER

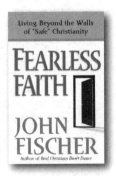

In our culture today, it's not always easy to be a Christian. It's natural to want to retreat into a "safe" subculture. Author and musician John Fischer challenges Christians to break out of the safety zone and engage others with the hope and promise of Jesus' good news. Through acts of compassion and honest, intelligent conversation, you can...

- meet and connect with skeptics and people who are looking for "something more"

- learn to recognize the ways God is already at work all around you

- change your world by becoming constructively involved in it

What Is Fact? What Is Fiction?
The Truth Behind the Da Vinci Code
RICHARD ABANES

"All descriptions of artwork, architecture, documents, and secret rituals in this novel are accurate."

With those startling words, *The Da Vinci Code*—author Dan Brown's megaselling thriller—kicks you into high gear. After 454 nonstop pages, you've discovered a lot of shocking facts about history and Christianity...or have you?

Award-winning investigative journalist Richard Abanes takes you down to the murky underpinnings of this blockbuster novel and movie that has confused so many people. What do you really learn when the *Code's* assumptions are unearthed and scrutinized?

- *The Code:* Jesus was married to Mary Magdalene, who he named leader of the church before his death.

- *The Truth:* This fantasy has no support even from the "Gnostic gospels" mentioned in the *Code*, let alone from the historical data.

- *The Code:* Since the year 1099, a supersecret society called "The Priory of Sion" has preserved knowledge of Jesus and Mary's descendants.

- *The Truth:* Today's "Priory of Sion"—— was founded in the early 1960s by a French con man who falsified documents to support the story of Jesus' "bloodline."

- *The Code:* As a "Priory" leader and pagan goddess-worshipper, Leonardo da Vinci coded secret knowledge about Jesus and Mary into his paintings.

- *The Truth:* Da Vinci had no known ties to any secret societies. Any obscure images in his paintings likely reflect his personal creativity.

Probing, factual, and revealing, *The Truth Behind the Da Vinci Code* gives you the straightforward information you need to separate the facts from the fiction.